KU-492-009

Love and Meaning in Religious Education

An Incarnational Approach to Teaching Christianity

D. J. O'Leary and T. Sallnow

NEWMAN COLLEGE
BARTLEY GREEN
BIRMINGHAM, 32.

CLASS	375.2
ACCESSION	74503
AUTHOR	OLE

WITHDRAWN

N 0006016 X

*To our parents brothers, sisters,
friends — with gratitude*

Oxford University Press, Walton Street, Oxford OX2 6DP

*London Glasgow New York Toronto
Delhi Bombay Calcutta Madras Karachi
Nairobi Dar es Salaam Cape Town Salisbury
Kuala Lumpar Singapore Hong Kong Tokyo
Melbourne Auckland*

and associate companies in
Beirut Berlin Ibadan Mexico City

© Oxford University Press 1982

Printed in Great Britain by Cambridge University Press, Cambridge

Contents

Prefaces

Introduction

PART ONE   **A Theology for the Incarnational Approach**

Chapter One   A Theology of Revelation
1.1   An Introduction to Incarnational Theology
1.2   The Contribution of Karl Rahner
1.3   Christ as the Revelation of God in Man
1.4   Grace as Interpersonal Reality
1.5   The Church as Sign-Community of the True World
1.6   The Sacraments as Celebrations of a New Humanity
1.7   The Eucharist as the Real Presence of Love in Creation
1.8   Original Sin as Fundamental to the Human Condition

Chapter Two   The Experience of Revelation
2.1   Revelation and Experience as Mutually Dependent
2.2   An Example from Doctrine
2.3   An Example from Liturgy
2.4   An Example from Man's Nature

PART TWO   **An Educational Theory for the Incarnational Approach**

Chapter Three   An Analysis of Meaning
3.1   The Contribution of Philip Phenix
3.2   Language and Meaning
3.3   Knowledge, Meaning and Experience

Chapter Four   Experience as 'Content' in Education

4.1   The Contribution of Kevin Nichols
4.2   Two Dimensions of Awareness in Experience
4.3   A Suggested Design for Religious Education

PART THREE   **A Curriculum Model for the Incarnational Approach**

Chapter Five   Curriculum Notes

5.1   Coherence and Structure in Curriculum Planning
5.2   Objectivity and Rationality in the New Structure
5.3   Curriculum Models and the Incarnational Approach
5.4   A Consideration of Aims
5.5   The Kingdom of Childhood and Incarnational Theology
5.6   The New Design as a Modern Apologetics
5.7   A Consideration of Objectives
5.8   The Place of Knowledge in Curriculum Planning
5.9   The Life-Theme in the New Design
5.10   A Theology for the Life-Theme
5.11   Structure and Sequence in the Life-Theme
5.12   An Observation on World Religions
5.13   Research and the R.E. Curriculum

Chapter Six   Preliminary Notes for a Work-Plan: an example

6.1   i) Introduction
6.2   ii) A Matter of Death and Life
Unit One   The Cathedral Will Rise Again
Unit Two   Out of the Ashes. . .
Unit Three   Unless the Grain of Wheat. . .
Unit Four   To Forgive is to Die a Little
Unit Five   Destroy This Temple. . .
Unit Six   As One Bread That is Broken. . .

Preface by Dr. Derek Webster

In *Witchita Vortex Sutra* Alan Ginsberg sees teachers as 'funky warlocks operating on guesswork'. Those who teach religious education know what he means for a key aspect of their subject, its theological dimension, is shadowy and barely articulated. This is sad for theology has a key role in shaping religious education. It provides an ideative focus for teachers. Their theological views affect the aims and objectives they set themselves, modify curricula content and flavour methodologies. Theology offers an understanding of reality that is crucial both to a self-understanding and to an apprehension of others. Not only is it important in strictly religious matters like the meaning of revelation, the nature of the church, the authority of the Bible and the engagement of major world religions, it is also evident as a value factor behind conceptual distinctions. Yet to affirm the importance of theology for religious education is not to fall into the trap of giving theological answers to educational questions or making educational criteria subserve theological ends. What is affirmed is the value of a robust dialogue between theology and education.

To embark on this dialogue is not to jeopardise the place of rationality or objectivity within religious education. It is to set them within a wider perspective. The truths of religions are only partly grasped by ratiocination. The inductive approach, despite its scientific respectability, gives a 'reality' which becomes normative too quickly. Yet the commitment of the religious person while related to this 'reality' is of a different order. Thus it is ironic that the reasoning which claims to explicate and evaluate religions draws back at just that boundary which the believer crosses in order to seek an 'other reality' — that to which he makes his commitment.

The dialogue between theology and education cannot be preset for its vigour depends upon its openness. It may be that it will address itself to the unfinished business of a previous generation by quickening in a contemporary context, epistemological questions. Those without and most of those with a religious commitment will not see theology as 'the queen of the sciences'. Yet from the believing perspective theology calls attention to that in the educational sciences which is inexplicable and ever mysterious; to those norms which stand outside the sciences and which are never self-justifying; to the fact that man is always the unanswered question. Theology prompts education to go beyond itself in the effort to glimpse the depths of that 'a priori' which stands behind all knowledge and which is antecedent to subject and object. Only because it is aware of its own provisional character, that it is all 'mere straw', does theology urge reason to wrestle with a mystery which it cannot grasp but which will grasp it, so that reason too may perceive its limiting boundaries. So it is that the believer, whatever his vision of the relationship of theology to other knowledge, always affirms the integration of all meaning into the reality of God.

Or it may be that the dialogue will deal exclusively with the difficulties and the opportunities of the present. A difficulty it might grasp concerns the view that psychological stage theory can account for religious development and spiritual maturation. This view, though widespread and supported by sophisticated theoretical models needs careful analysis. Theology might ask whether or not a self-consistent, universal, invariant and hierarchical sequence of stages characterises spiritual growth for experience suggests that it does not. There seems to be incongruity between what the theory suggests and what life shows. Further problems are evident as theology reflects on the definitions offered for the stage structures. It seems unlikely that the highest stages of spiritual growth can be defined in operational terms when the mystery they refer to is neither conceptually nor existentially exhausted.

An opportunity which the dialogue might seize is a consideration of the processes of knowing as these concern the imaginitive and the creative aspects of human life. For it is arguable that there is behind the discernment and communication of the truth of our experiences, a grammar or a key pattern generating and structuring knowledge. It seems that this pattern is characterised less by rational processes and more by conflicts which provoke imaginative and creative moves of thought, moves which often appear to be 'given' within an individual's thinking. From the side of commitment a believer might see here space created for the movement of the Holy Spirit.

A further opportunity and really one of the most important ones in terms of its practical effects, is the one developed by the authors of this book. They offer a careful and refreshing rationale for a contemporary religious education which takes a proper account of the role of theology. Here there is a genuine engagement between education and theology. Each is allowed to speak at profound levels, though neither one is permitted to dominate at the expense of the other. The 'incarnational approach' proposes a religious education which is securely based. Its methodology and content are ecumenical; the width of its argument is impressive; the extent of its application unlimited. Teachers able to see the roots of their subject at last will gain a new confidence and young people encouraged to discern the depths within their own experience may see the meaning of their lives enhanced.

It is impossible to read this book fairly without reflecting on and reassessing one's own practice in religious education. Its authors proffer an invitation to their readers to share in a collective enterprise of quarrying ideas and constructing structures. The enterprise promises greater self knowledge and a clearer and much more exciting understanding of what religious education can be. Here then is a key document in the struggle to fashion the subject for our own times, a document which is, adapting the words of Bernard Lonergan, attentive, intelligent, reasonable, responsible and loving.

D. H. Webster

Preface by Monsignor Kevin Nichols

'Where there is much desire to learn, there of necessity will be much arguing, much writing, many opinions; for opinion in good men is but knowledge in the making'. The eloquence of Milton's impassioned plea for freedom of speech remains fresh. We are right to be grateful that his campaign has borne fruit; that in a substantial part of the world people are no longer afraid to speak in an open and forthright way of matters they care about. Without this freedom we shall not learn. At least we are unlikely to learn the truth.

Over the last half-century or so, there has certainly been a great deal of writing and argument about religious education both inside and outside the Christian community. Much progress has been made. Yet the authors of this book often write as though they feel themselves to be still at the beginning of an immense task which stretches a great distance into the future. And indeed, when we consider the development and renewal of religious education, at least within the Roman Catholic community, we have an impression of a good deal of skating on thin ice. New things are being done but for reasons which sometimes seem half understood. About them hangs, faintly, the air of a night battle. What is the reason for this?

Perhaps it is to be found in three things: a lack of depth, a lack of completeness, a lack of synthesis. The seeds of many hopeful ideas are snatched by the birds or simply fall by the wayside because there is no ground of intellectual dialogue at some depth to receive them; because they can find no lodgement in the commonwealth of learnings. The preparation of such ground is indeed a complex task. To engage in it however is to meet with much impatience on the part of practitioners, of parents and of leaders of institutions. This impatience is understandable especially when it comes from parents who are worried about their children. Yet it would be foolish to sacrifice long-term gains for the sake of the immediate. Moreover only conditioning or indoctrination can be guaranteed to produce with certainty the outcomes which are wanted. Procedures which are educational respect the person, his individuality and his growth and are therefore never foolproof. Education is a risky business.

In the face of these difficulties, two tempting but false trails are sometimes followed. The first is the attempt to deduce a basic theory of religious education directly from theological premisses. This, while it may result in a body of content-material to be taught, rarely makes fruitful contact with the educational process. The other is the attempt to work out a notion of 'pure education', sterilised of values and kept in a cool, dry, germ-free place. Theoretically acceptable to all, this often proves welcome to none. Whatever nice distinctions may be made, Christians inescapably find that the inner logic of their faith is woven into their educational thinking.

The groundwork of religious education must relate the insights of theology and philosophy of education. It must comprehend development psychology and the techniques of curriculum development. It must resolve, or at least hold in balance the responsibility of a believing community to catechise, that is to initiate new members; and the responsibility of society at large to establish a common norm of education which must be observed by all those who participate in its procedures. This network of related material could not be held together in a theoretical synthesis. The study of education yields rather a practical theory whose notional unity is looser. Its focus is a practical activity rather than an abstract scheme.

Among the elements in this synthesis, theology has usually been the weakest. It is for that reason that this book is so important. Its authors have taken as their starting-point and a major part of their substance, incarnational theology as exemplified in the work of Karl Rahner. Working this out, especially in their theology of revelation, they have moved it towards educational theory and practice. They push all of this forward to show how it can be developed into a basic theory of curriculum; and they offer examples of how this curriculum theory would work out in practice. They construct a process of educational thought which does justice to many different considerations; a model which provides stability, yet allows for development both in theology and in educational studies. Along with this working model they offer a substantial piece of practical theology which will be of great interest to many people and will be influential in the continuing renewal of religious education. I very much hope that their book will be widely read and discussed.

Kevin Nichols.
Our Lady's.
Washington
Tyne & Wear.

Introduction

Like a stream, now placid even sluggish, now suddenly troubled by flood-waters as swollen tributaries pour into it their eager currents, the history of Christian theology has developed, sometimes slowly, sometimes violently. The present century has seen its fair share of such progress and consequent agitation particularly in Roman Catholic and Anglican circles. To a somewhat lesser extent the same observations are valid for approaches to religious education. The Education Act of 1944, for instance, stimulated unprecedented comment in this field. During the past few decades a high level of research has generally been maintained and many educationalists have explored in depth the theoretical and methodological dimensions of the subject within perspectives varying from the confessional to the phenomenological.

Progress there certainly has been at a theoretical level in these separate disciplines. But few people concerned with Christian education today are content with the present state of classroom R.E. In Church schools or Local Authority schools, there is much cause for concern. Recent research has produced little reason for complacency.[1] As a matter of fact, at the present moment it is difficult to exaggerate the precarious state of R.E. in general and the teaching of the Christian religion in particular. To a large extent this worrying situation is due to the fact that while there have been tremendous developments, on the one hand in the area of theology and on the other in the sphere of educational theory, there have been relatively few attempts to synthesise these two in an approach to religious education. At a time when a pluralism in theology and educational theory prevails, there is little evidence of serious effort to structure new curriculum aims and objectives in terms of this richness. Indeed, many contemporary R.E. syllabuses seem to be uninfluenced by any one significant theological pos-

---

(1) FRANCES, L. *Christianity and the Child To-day*: A Research Perspective on the situation in England (Occasional Papers, The Farmington Institute for Christian Studies. No. 6. E. Hulmes ed.)

ition or by current views in the area of curriculum theory. The resulting disenchantment with the subject may be due, in part, to this neglect. It is worth reminding ourselves again that 'the religious educator is at once theologian and educator, for the field of religious education is located at the point where theology and education intersect.'[2] In this book we are attempting an initial step in the direction of such a synthesis by examining the implications for religious education of adopting a particular theology and a particular educational theory. 'The problem is to detect that ground where a contemporary theology will resonate with a modern educational theory.'[3]

While respecting the valuable contribution of certain contemporary trends in speculative theology, many of them still comparatively new and untested, we have decided to work within a context of the current renewal in traditional and classical theism, central to Christianity and resting on deep historical truths and profound scholarship. In Part One we attempt to provide a few examples of what we mean by the term 'Incarnational Theology' which belongs to the 'neo-orthodox' model of systematic theology in modern Christian research.[4] After much reflection and con- sultation it seems clear to us that the starting point of our whole presen- tation must be in this area. The authors of *Religious Education in Primary Schools*, for instance, seem keenly aware of the theological turmoil that has arisen in the wake of the 'Life-Theme' approach to R.E. 'We recog- nise,' they write, 'that this new kind of religious education requires in teachers a high degree of theological insight. . .'[5] In the Introduction (p.4) and in their Recommendations (p.69) they press for clarification regarding the 'theological presuppositions of the thematic approach.' The Incarnational approach is the name we give to a design for R.E. where the emergence of the life of the world is not radically re-cast but purified by revelation; where human experience is not suppressed or basically drawn

---

(2) McBRIEN, R. *Catholicism* (Chapman, 1980), p. 29
(3) WEBSTER, D. *Creativity within Religious Education*: A note towards the Significance for Religious Education of a Dialogue between Christian Theology and Humanistic Psychology (article in British Journal of Religious Education, Vol. 2, No. 4, 1980)
(4) For recent attempts to identify basic models and approaches in contemporary theology cf. TRACY, D. *Blessed Rage for Order* (Seabury Press, 1975) pp. 22–32, and McBrien, R. op. cit., pp. 56–61.
(5) *Religious Education in Primary Schools*: Schools Council Working Paper 44 (Evans/Methuen Educational, 1972: p. 63); In many of their writings over the past decade Hull, J. and Grimmitt, M. concern themselves with these issues. See also articles in *Christianity in the Classroom* (C.E. in 1978 by Birnie, I. and Hinton, M.)

out of shape but revealed in its true nature by the event of Incarnation. It is in the absence of an approach which accomplishes or even comes to grips with this synthesis where violence is done to neither God nor man, that the present approach is being proposed. This whole exercise bristles with difficulties and requires careful study. Some sections in Chapter One (section ii) for example, may be seen as making firm demands on the attention of the busy reader. It seems to us that this challenge is necessary since we are dealing here with the acquisition of new vision and perspective rather than with reformulations within familiar patterns.

Part Two contains reflections on the merits and de-merits of recent thinking on the nature of education, meaning, communication and curriculum design both in education in general and R.E. in particular.[6] It searches for common ground between a theory of education, of man, and of revelation that provides a unified basis for a dynamic approach to R.E. The aim here is to compare philosophical models of the curriculum by way of integrating cognition and meaning on the basis of the central Incarnational approach dealt with in Part One. In addition there is some discussion of the symbolic, mediating and sometimes limited character of language which points up the importance of other creative forms of learning and communication in the curriculum (e.g. Art, Music, Movement) and the necessity of existential terminology in R.E. as the means of opening up the truth encapsulated in doctrinal and scriptural concepts. There is exploration, too, into the value of story and fantasy as vehicles of meaning for the integrated development of the child.

In Part Three we make suggestions for ways and means of applying the various strands of the arguments and positions adopted in the preceding sections, in the interests of clarifying an approach to a particular curriculum structure. The book ends with some representative examples of how selected themes might be developed practically in a new R.E. curriculum-plan.[7]

---

(6)   For excellent examples and surveys of development and design in this area cf. GOLDBY, M. (ed.) *Curriculum Design* (Croom Helm: 1975) and HOOPER, R. (ed.). *The Curriculum; Context, Design and Development* (Oliver & Boyd, 1971); Lawton, D. et al. *Theory and Practice of Curriculum Studies* (Routledge & Keegan Paul, 1978)
(7)   There is an obvious need for many more initiatives in education programmes concerned with exploration into experience in terms of both the literary and the creative arts. cf. LEALMAN, B. and ROBINSON, E. *The Image of Life* (Christian Education Movement, 1980)

PART ONE

A Theology for the Incarnational Approach

Chapter One   A Theology of Revelation

1.1   An Introduction to Incarnational Theology

'God became man so that man could become God.' The early Fathers of the Church never tired of repeating this and similar phrases. The clarity of their vision was obscured in the subesquent history of Christianity and a precious element of revelation was thus neglected. This book is an effort to restore the centrality of one basic Christian insight into the relationship between divine grace and human experience and to suggest how a renewal of this emphasis could affect our approach to religious education.

All too often theologians and religious educators subscribe to an 'extrinsicist' view of Christian Revelation where redemption is seen exclusively as a kind of rescue operation on God's part – an intervention from the outside to salvage a world gone adrift. The popular theology of the past few centuries tended to regard grace as a kind of superstructure on the foundation of nature – an added extra divine icing to an already formed but incomplete human cake. Much of this Manichean and Gnostic type of emphasis can be traced to a view of Incarnation which sees God as simply and absolutely superior to the material world, drawing near to it in order to save it, meeting the spirit of the world in order to change its radically distinct nature.[1] This view is basically heretical, yet it has deeply coloured the Christian approach to religious education in many significant ways. Doctrine and dogmas, for instance, were often seen as ready-made truths about God, left behind by Christ, for men to contemplate. A static view of revelation prevailed. Religious education was primarily concerned with the transmission of a deposit of divine secrets received from outside and preserved for the future in a 'deposit' of faith.

After a lean and barren period in the history of Christian theological thought a new dynamism has entered the notion of revelation. No longer is

---

(1)   Manichaeism and Gnosticism were influential in the third century. Both systems of belief are recognizable as Christian deviations, advocating an acute dualism where matter and the physical body were regarded as evil. Before his conversion St. Augustine spent nine years as a member of the Manichee sect. Irenaeus vigorously opposed all such movements regarding them in his writings as anti-Incarnational.

it considered as a collection of objective propositions which themselves tended to become the object of faith. Inhibitive of growth and freedom, concerned not with a living God and living men but with a Deity who has retired from the world leaving his truths behind him, much traditional theology has often robbed faith of its inner life. Emphasis today is on revelation as a process rather than a product and as a personal enrichment rather than a passive reception of impersonal data. The view of revelation currently finding support, as the initial insight of the early Fathers is gradually being recaptured, regards it as indicating the divine element inherent in all authentic human experience rather than as non-historical and non-social interventions from without. Revelation is now seen to be about the unfolding to man of the true nature of his own already-graced life and of the unforeseen possibilities intrinsic to his own humanity.

The Incarnational approach to religious education argues that if the central notion of salvation, as revealed fully and only in Christ, is that all creation speaks of God, then God is revealed in the 'letting be of being' when all creatures are allowed to be themselves and to emerge along the lines of their own true nature. 'The more that things are true to themselves, the more truly they reflect the glory of God. God's revelation is not a religious veneer on things nor a religious message to be injected into people . . . I cannot approach the non-believer or the child with the assumption that he has not been touched by God's grace. I cannot assume that my task is to fill an empty vessel or that I possess something with which the vessel is to be filled. I can only approach the other with an attitude of invitation that we take up the quest together, for the God already active in our lives.'[2]

The Incarnational approach is concerned with presenting to pupils a view of revelation as that which contributes in a specific and singular way to each person's self-understanding. Christian revelation is seen in terms of its unprecedented contribution to a pupil's personal discovery as he searches for a meaning to his life. This contribution, optimistic yet realistic, is a truth that has become evident in Christ. It establishes the fact for the Christian that God has so made the universe that he can only be encountered by man in all his experiences within that universe. The implication for R.E. and for education in its broadest sense is the central emphasis on the reasons for the respect and reverence that all growing and emerging life demands. 'Since God's revelation comes to full expression in human life,

---

(2)   MORAN, G. *Vision and Tactics* (Herder & Herder, 1968) p. 24

it is henceforth life with all its ambiguities and lack of rationality that becomes the norm.'[3] One of the results of this approach to R.E. will be the recognition of creation as precisely creation — not as a plan that went wrong, a means to an end, or a threatening situation from which to be set free. Creation is set in the context of gift rather than threat, of opportunity rather than test. Revelation is seen as the affirmation of humanity by shedding light on the dark mystery of suffering and growth.

It might be useful at this point to cite a number of key thinkers in whose work this understanding of revelation can be traced. While holding quite separate, and sometimes almost opposing, views D. Bonhoeffer, P. Tillich and K. Rahner, have, between them, contributed largely to a redefinition and a re-introduction of an exciting dimension of theology that has an immediate attraction for men in search of meaning and fulfilment. The strength and weakness of their approaches have been associated with their efforts to link the Christian Gospel to a particular expression of modern philosophy. The objectivity of the historical beginning of the Church together with its corporate experience and its accumulated traditions is in danger of being eroded, many fear, in the emphasis on existentialism as a new companion for theology. We will return to the merits of this valuable objection in the consideration of the central place occupied by the Incarnation in the existential and life-centred approach of these men.

The kind of language used about God by the authors in question points to an ultimate relatedness in the very structure of man's being from which there is no escape. 'This kind of God-language,' J.A.T. Robinson writes, 'is a way of keeping guard over the irreducible, ineffable mystery at the heart of all experience. Traditionally, theology — our map of this mystery — has depicted God at the frontier of human existence. But this has come to mean for most people today something at the periphery of their experience or beyond it.'[4]

He concludes that Christians must work towards a projection that re-centres the reality of God, not at the boundaries of life where human powers fail, but, as Bonhoeffer demanded, at its centre and strength, as the 'beyond in the midst.' For today's theologians of 'the new school', reality, whether looked at from the outside or the inside, is all of a piece. They will not entertain a dualistic model of the universe. For them, Robinson explains 'there is no second storey to the universe, no realm of the divine

---

(3)   MORAN ibid p. 26
(4)   ROBINSON, J. *Exploration into God* (S.C.M., 1967) p. 72

over and above or behind the processes of nature and history which perforates this world or breaks it by supernatural intervention. The traditional divisions with which theology has worked — body and soul, earth and heaven, this world and the other world, the secular and the sacred — are decreasingly viable or useful. They are categories that have ceased to speak to the consciousness of modern man, who no longer does his thinking in them. . . '[5] The implication of this is not, of course, the abolition of the transcendent in pure naturalism, nor a deification of the natural as some popularisers would suggest: it is an apprehension of the transcendent as given in, with, and under the immanent. In this 'shot-silk' universe the 'beyond' is to be found only 'in the midst' as a function and dimension of it. At this point Robinson quotes H. Cox and we shall see later why he suggests that the latter is re-echoing his eminent Catholic elders, T. de Chardin and K. Rahner, when he writes: 'Man, seen as the steersman of the cosmos, is the only starting point we have for a viable doctrine of God.'[6]

Bonhoeffer's understanding of revelation reflects the central thrust of the Incarnational approach. As with Bultmann, he is often misrepresented. To regard his reasons for adopting the phrase 'religionless Christianity' as a basis for 'religionless R.E.' is to caricature his theology. For him, as for Bultmann, Christ was central, but Christ made *flesh*. All his thinking stemmed from one centre — the revelation of God in Jesus Christ — and every utterance is in the end a Christocentric utterance. ' . . . in Christ we are offered the possibility of partaking in the reality of God and in the reality of the world but not in the one without the other.'[7] The inner meaning of revelation is that when man encounters the reality of the world, it is already constituted in the reality of God. The 'religion' he railed against was a false pietism concerned only with the salvation of the soul — a sector of life, so to speak, where God could come into his own. God is removed from the centre of the world and Christ is made into an object of religion. But God can be reached only through the world and adored within it. 'I am still discovering up to this very moment', Bonhoeffer wrote, 'that it is only by living completely in this world that one learns to believe.'[8]

How many programme-planners have seriously attempted to encapsulate this vision into a new design for R.E.? The essence of the Incarnational

---

(5)   ROBINSON *op. cit.* pp. 78f
(6)   COX, H. *The Secular City Debate* p. 199, quoted in Robinson, *op. cit.* p. 79
(7)   BONHOEFFER, D. *Ethics* (Macmillan, 1955), p. 161.
(8)   MOLTMANN & WEISSBACH *Two Studies in the Theology of Bonhoeffer* (Scribners, 1967) p. 121

approach is caught up in these words — 'The purpose and aim of the domination of Christ is not to make the worldly order godly, or to subordinate it to the Church but to set it free for true worldliness.'[9] Since statements such as these conflict with a conventional (but not with a truly traditional) Christian outlook, we will attempt to find support for them in the theological anthropology of K. Rahner (below). Genuine worldliness for D. Bohoeffer means 'allowing the world to be what it really is before God. . . '[10] By 'worldliness' he did not mean 'the shallow this-worldliness of the enlightened, of the busy, the comfortable, the lascivious. It is something much more profound than that, something in which the knowledge of death and resurrection is ever present. . .'[11] In his thinking here, Bonhoeffer is concerned with the two meanings of 'world' as reflected in the Gospel of John. It was because of his insight into the meaning of the fleshing of God, the humanity of the Word and the vulnerability of the Son that Bonhoeffer could say of *all* human activity; 'In the events themselves is God.'[12] Tomorrow's R.E. programme-planners for teaching Christianity, whether 'experientially' or 'explicitly', will have to carefully familiarise themselves with this elusive tension between God, man and Christ. The wisdom within revelation makes a slow and bloody entrance into the mind of man.

1.2   The Contribution of Karl Rahner

Karl Rahner too is one of the most significant philosophical theologians of our time. What follows is a brief but, for our purpose, adequate summary of his prolific and often difficult writings regarding the sacred and the secular. We will endeavour to concentrate on the finely-balanced tension between the two aspects of Incarnational theology that we already briefly traced in the theology of Bonhoeffer and others — the tension between nature and grace where neither element dominates or surrenders to the other, but where both are mutually established in an inseparable union. Rahner holds, with Bultmann, that it is not possible to speak theologically about God without at the same time saying something about man and vice versa. A theology centred on man is not in opposition to a theology centred on Christ. In Christian theology there is a mutual and necessary relation-

---

(9)   BONHOEFFER *op. cit.* p. 294
(10)   BONHOEFFER *op. cit.* p. 165
(11)   BONHOEFFER *Letters and Papers from Prison* (Fontana, 1950) p. 169
(12)   BONHOEFFER *ibid.* quoted by Moltmann and Weissbach op. cit. p. 114

ship between anthropology and Christology. Christian anthropology only attains its full meaning when it conceives of man as the openness and capacity for union with God, or as 'the obediential potency for the hypo-static union.'[1] The Incarnation occurred not because creation went wrong at some stage, but because creation was necessary for Incarnation to happen. 'There is no difficulty in thinking that the first, primal and comprehensively eternal will of God is his own self-expression and that in this act of will, God wills the humanity of Christ and hence creation in general as its setting.'[2] The plea is for a shift in emphasis akin to the 'Blondelian shift'[3] as G. Baum and G. Moran refer to it, where the secular is seen in terms of emergence, growth and identity, and the sacred is seen as one of the great forces which will compel the secular to be truly itself. 'We could still say of the Creator, with the Scripture of the Old Testament, that he is in heaven and we are on earth. But of the God whom we confess in Christ we must say that he is precisely where we are, and can only be found there.'[4] Creation is already constituted in grace because it is, so to speak, the rough-draft of the shape of God. The Incarnational approach is based on the simple truth of faith that 'what we call sanctifying grace and divine life is present everywhere — wherever, in fact, man does not close himself to the God of salvation. . . For we know that this grace is being communicated, even though in ways that are partially anonymous and hidden, within the concrete reality and history of human life: and we know that grace is present wherever the struggle of human living and dying takes its course. From its inmost roots, from the inmost personal centre of each spiritual grace, upheld and borne along by God's subjects, the world is constantly seized by self-communication .'[5]

The event of Incarnation only explicates in the light what is already afoot and hidden within human existence from the first creation. The calling into existence of the concrete world is from the beginning and by

---

(1)   RAHNER *Theological Investigations Vol. IX* (Darton, Longman & Todd, 1972) p. 2
(2)   RAHNER *Theological Investigations Vol. IV* (Darton, Longman & Todd, 1964) p. 213
(3)   BLONDEL, Maurice (d. 1949) was a French philosopher and theologian. His position concerning the Christian revelation, called 'The method of immanence' anticipated the work of many leading contemporary theologians, cf. BAUM, G. *Man Becoming* (Herder & Herder, 1970) Ch. 1
(4)   RAHNER op. cit. p. 117
(5)   RAHNER *Secular Life and the Sacraments* (The Tablet, Vol. 225, No. 6822 March, 1971) p. 237

definition, an implicit Christianity. With hindsight we can now see that
the implicit has become explicit. It is only to the eyes of faith then, that
the smallest particle of creation becomes a theophany and a revelation.
'Through every cleft, the world we perceive floods us with riches — food
for the body, nourishment for the eyes, the harmony of sounds and fullness of the heart, unknown phenomena and new truths — all these treasures,
all these stimuli, all these calls coming to us from the four corners of the
world, cross our consciousness at every moment. What is their role within
us? They will merge into the most intimate life of our soul, and either
develop it or poison it.'[6] Robinson recognises the similarity of insight and
argumentation between these words of the Jesuit scientist and the 'God
as depth' conclusions of Tillich, since he is fully aware of the Incarnational
centre of the profound thinking of these men. Many contemporary 'Suggestions' and 'Groundplans' for R.E. fight shy of revealing the Christocentric
nature of this approach to life in the actual working-out of their themes,
but the prefaces and introductions almost invariably testify to a commitment to the conclusions reached by 'the new theologians.' There is a strange
(but in the light of the history of Church education, understandable)
reluctance to clarify the fact that 'the inmost dynamism of what has been
known at all times and in every place as man's ordinary 'profane' existence
has found at a particular point in time and space its clearest manifestation
and meaning in Jesus of Nazareth.[7]

Two Views of Incarnation

This needs further clarification. It can be argued, according to Rahner, that
God created the world, in the first place, as a remote preparation for the
coming of Christ. To understand creation then, we must be aware of the
uniqueness of the Incarnation, and see both these mysteries in terms of
revelation. 'What is chronologically first', writes Moran, 'must be understood in the light of the later, full revelation.'[8]

An 'extrinsicist' view of the relationship between the creation of the
world and the Incarnation of the Word would see God's intervention in
human affairs as 'from outside.' God spoke to men from afar, conveying to
them through the prophets, truths in human statements, directions and

---

(6)   de CHARDIN *Le Milieu Divin* (Collins, 1960) p. 59
(7)   RAHNER *The Church and the Sacraments* (Burns & Oates, 1963) p. 15
(8)   MORAN, G. *Theology of Revelation* (Search Press, 1966) p. 61

commandments, in preparation for the entry of His Son. Between God and man there was no intrinsic link; the connection between the grace of faith and historical revelation was either very tenuous or non-existent. This view tends to see human nature as something used by God to make himself visible and audible. 'We must, therefore, regard as heretical any concept of the Incarnation which makes the humanity of Jesus only a disguise used by God to signal his challenging presence.'[9] Incarnation would then appear as a superstructure over nature and consciousness, arbitrarily erected – a platform on which fallen man was offered a second chance. This theory does not affirm the substantial unity of God's presence and human nature, due to a faulty understanding of the gratuity of grace, the immutability of God and the meaning of creation. (cf. Fig. 1.)

An alternative theology, however, endeavours to answer the following questions: can we say that revelation, while of immediate divine origin, is also the heart of human history; how does the history of revelation and the history of salvation relate to the basic history of spiritual man realising his own identity and destiny? How do we account for the 'scandal of particularity' in which revelation, present everywhere from the beginning, finds partial expression in certain prophets and full expression in one particular man? Rahner offers a statement not immediately concerned with revelation, but one which will serve as an outline to be developed. 'It might be suggested,' he writes, 'that the most general relation between God and a mutable world consists in the fact that God, as most immanent – and yet for that reason absolutely superior to the world – confers on finite beings themselves a true active self-transcendence in their change and becoming and is himself ultimately the future, the final cause, which represents the true and really effective cause, operative in all change.'[10] Rahner is endeavouring to show that revelation is not concerned with the making known of something over-against man but with man's own growing awareness of his spiritual destiny. Contrary to the extrinsicist position, God's decree, elevating man to the supernatural order, produces an intrinisic ontological effect on man's human nature, so that from the beginning it is graced with the possibility of becoming divine. 'God became man so that man could become God.' (cf. Fig. 1.)

(9)   RAHNER *Theological Investigations Vol. IV* (op. cit.) p. 117f
(10)   RAHNER & RATZINGER *Revelation and Tradition* (Burns & Oates, 1965)
p. 12

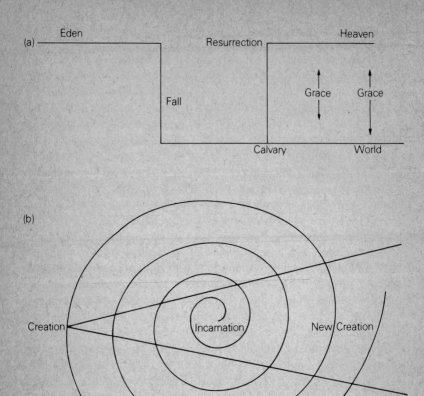

Figure 1: Two models of Revelation-theology

Self-Transcending Man

At this stage a short summary might help. Because God is love, he wished to express that love. His whispered word we call the Logos. But this loving word had to be uttered to someone, and so, man was created. Moreover, man had to be created so that he could hear the word of love, accept (or refuse) the offer, and accept or refuse it freely as the gift that it is. Because

God wished to become identified with the created object of his love (which he eventually did), he had to create a being who was capable of this unique union, a being with a congeniality and desire for 'the longest stride of soul men ever took.' Man is called into being so that love might transform him by bestowing itself. This readiness, this aptitude, this demand almost, is what Rahner calls man's 'obediential potency' and constitutes what is inmost and most authentic in him, the centre and root of what he absolutely and always is. This resumé is simple. It is based in man's experience of himself who desires, in freedom, to be known and loved. And the outcome of his condition was speculative until the Logos and human nature united in mutual love to such an extent that God, in fact, became man. This is the theological support for what we have called the Incarnational approach.

Man is spirit in that he lives life in a continual reaching out towards God. Rahner claims that it belongs to man's fundamental make-up to be the absolute openness for being as such. Man continually transcends everything in the pursuit and realisation of his own becoming. This openness to the future is not a contingency which can emerge here or there at will in man but is 'the condition for the possibliity of that which man is and has to be. . . The only thing which makes him a man is that he is forever on the road to God.'[11] He is the infinite openness of the finite for God. Man's condition is intially so structured as to be that part of creation, which can reach beyond itself and by being transformed into God himself by its capacity for receiving the divine self-communication, be a revelation, in time of the very essence of God. 'God's creative act always drafts the creature as the paradigm of a possible utterance of himself.'[12] Man has an ever-open ear for every word of God. Each passing moment and each chance encounter contains a question for man. The Incarnational appoach to the life-theme is concerned with the quality of one's listening and the accuracy of one's interpretation. It examines man's resistance to reality and self-knowledge, his guilt and anxieties, and points out that these are the diseases from which the Christian hopes to be liberated. Again and again in the dialogue and communion that are central to all human experience, man is addressed by the painful word that evokes a response of affirmation and so transforms life, or a negative reaction that diminishes growth. The uttered Word of God makes man a listener. To be a hearer of the Word is to be unconditionally open to reality and to the perception of the truth.

---

(11) RAHNER *Hearers of the Word* (Sheed and Ward, 1969) p. 66
(12) RAHNER *Theological Investigations Vol. IV* (op. cit.) p. 115

Christ the True Man

A clarifying word on the central place of Christ, on whom the preceding arguments are based, will conclude this section. When it is said that God's revelation reaches its highest moment in Christ, or, put in another way, that the free possible act of revelation of God encounters man who recognises it in freedom, more is meant than the fact that Christ was the end of the 'line of promise', that he was the last and greatest of the prophets, or that his words and miracles were unique. He is not the bearer of revelation; he *is* the revelation. Revelation is more than a series of truths about God to be understood by man; it is a person. He is, in person, the message he brings. Christ does not merely utter words about God; he himself is the uttered word. The person of Christ is regarded as the summit and full reality of creation. He is the explanation of life, 'the surfacing of meaning' as J. Robinson expressed it. Every moment of his life was an invitation to become more, or less, human. In fact, he never said 'no' to any opportunity to grow. Always open to love, he never compromised. To discover what man ought to be, what man can be, the Christian looks at Christ because he reveals the true man. He reveals, first of all, that man is born to live in relationship, not in isolation. Christ is not the abnormal man: he is the norm, we the abnormal. He is the concentric, we are the eccentric; he is the true, we are out of true. 'He does not reveal,' writes H. Lavery, 'what it is to be divine; he reveals what it is to be human. And he reveals that we are not human beings but human becomings. That we are not born human; we become human or sub-human.'[13] That all men might become god-like is the purpose of creation. The Christian believes that his attitude to every experience of his day either nourishes or poisons that potential.

From 'man's side,' the achievement of the Incarnation means that in Christ the nature of man allowed itself to be grasped by the incomprehensible. His hunger was given meaning; his emptiness filled. From 'God's side,' it means that in Christ God's creative love, which led him to utter his first self-disposing Word, the Logos, at the very beginning of time — and which led him too, as we have just noted, both to create man and to create within him the possibility of accepting this ever present Word — has found, at last, a permanent and complete home here on earth. In Christ, man's nature has been assumed by God as his own reality, and so has arrived (but only in this unique man and only too by virtue of God's free grace) at the union

---

(13) LAVERY, H. *Why Sacraments?* (Uniscripts, No. 9: Upholland Northern Institute, 1978) part I: p. 1

for which it has always longed and striven. In Christ it was forever established that the meaning of man lay in his transcendence and receptivity towards God – a potential that anticipated a perfection that could be neither
demanded or merited by man, but which did in fact take place in Christ. It
is because Christ is the fulness of man's self-surrender to the mystery of
God's self-communicating grace that we can refer to him as the fulness of
revelation. We can enlarge on this by holding that in Christ human nature
belongs so little to itself (continually self-transcending in pursuit of its destiny) that it becomes the nature of God himself. 'The incarnation of God
is the unique, supreme case of the total actualisation of human reality
which consists of the fact that man is in so far as he gives himself up.'[14]

Christ completed and perfected what creation began by being at once
'the way forward' for the final and irrevocable break-through of man into
God and 'the way in' for the ever-approaching, self-disposing love of God
for man. He was too, the ultimate locus for the consummation of these two
movements – a consummation that summed up all that was graced potential in man – making him the first of men whose own existence throws
light on the true meaning of created humanity.

'In Jesus of Nazareth the self-communicating presence of the mystery
we name 'God' and our personal quest reach the highest level of intensity:
they meet never to be separate; they meet as one. Jesus is subjective human
personhood and subjective divinity as one. On the one hand, the self-
disclosure of God driven by love pushes outward until God becomes the object of His love – a human being. At the same time the self-transcendence
and religious openness characteristic of each man and woman find a special
intensity in Jesus of Nazareth.'[15]

The immanence of the word, now, for men, is the address of the
Spirit. 'Grace is simply the last depth and the radical meaning of all that
the created person experiences, enacts and suffers in the process of developing and realising himself as a person. When someone experiences laughter
or tears, bears responsibility, stands by the truth, breaks through the egoism in his life with other people; where someone hopes against hope, faces
the shallowness and stupidity of the daily rush and bustle with humour
and patience, refusing to become embittered; where someone learns to be
silent and in this inner silence lets the evil in his heart die rather than spread

---

(14)   RAHNER *Theological Investigations Vol. IV* (op. cit.) p. 110
(15)   O'MEARA, T.F. *Theology of Revelation* (article in Theological Studies,
September, 1975) p. 422

outwards; in a word, wherever someone lives as he would like to live, combating his own egoism and the continual temptation to inner despair — there is the event of grace.'[16]

1.3   Christ as the Revelation of God in Man

Jesus Christ, the Perfect Man

For a long while the Christological debate has revolved around such issues as the relation of the divine and human natures in Christ, the levels of his knowledge and self-consciousness, and the various theories of atonement. Our corresponding theology of revelation has tended to reflect a similar rather essentialist character: Christ is the revelation of God and it is in him that revelation attains its perfection and fullness. But this statement is generally understood in a more or less propositional way, our interpretation of revelation remaining on the level of something objectively delivered to man in the form of a collection of divine truths transmitted through Christ's words and actions. The implication is that our task is to appropriate these established truths as they have been handed on through the post-apostolic Church. This is of course true in a sense, but it can also lend itself to an extremely limited understanding of Incarnation. Life, death, and the continual hope of a new and deeper knowledge of self and existence are pervasive and unavoidable elements of human consciousness and experience. It is no accident that these very elements constitute the core of Christian faith in that they are gathered up and heightened to perfection in the man Jesus Christ. If Christian revelation is about God — a God who is not alien or absent — then equally it must be about man, for in Christ is united the divine offer of love and complete human receptivity. The locus of revelation therefore is the living experience of humanity and its meaning in the light of Christ. 'The truth is that only in the mystery of the incarnate Word does the mystery of man take on light. For Adam, the first man, was a figure of Him who was to come, namely, Christ the Lord. Christ, the final Adam, by the revelation of the mystery of the Father and His love, fully reveals man to man himself and makes his supreme calling clear. It is not surprising, then, that in Him all the aforementioned truths find their root and attain their crown. . . . He blazed a trail, and if we

---

(16)   RAHNER *Secular Life and the Sacraments* (op. cit.) p. 237

follow it, life and death are made holy and take on a new meaning.'[1]

Jesus Christ is the summit of the history of man's self-discovery; he is not qualitatively different from the human race, but is rather the fullest expression of self-actualisation which is the vocation and potential of *all* men, by virtue of their createdness in God's image. 'The light that appeared in Jesus,' observes Bultmann, 'is none other than that which had already shone forth in creation.'[2] In Christ, the law of human evolution has come to fulfilment; in him humanity's quest for 'being-human-in-God', as Hubert Halbfas puts it[3], has found its goal; in him man has overcome his fallenness. The big evolutionary breakthrough has happened: the man Jesus Christ has demonstrated the ultimate power of true loving as a real possibility for all, not simply as one amongst many stages in the evolution of the world, but as the highest point towards which everything is in movement. The triumph of love has been assured, not just in relation to the man Jesus himself, but in terms of every man, in all cultures throughout the history of the world. 'Jesus came to reveal to us in a superabundance how loving is the fundamental power in the universe. . . . He came to tell us that we need not fear, that we could take the risk of vulnerability required by loving reconciliation. Thus it is in and through Jesus as the revelation of the loving trustworthiness of God (and the cosmos and life he has created) that we overcome the effects of the sin of the human race.'[4]

Some of the most forceful Scriptural statements of the nature of Christian revelation are undoubtedly those uttered by Pilate in the Passion Narratives: 'Behold the man . . . I can find no fault in him.' Here is an assertion of Incarnation on the part of one who had also asked, 'Truth — what is truth?' His own words were the answer. Behold *the* authentic man, whose full and total acceptance of life and death, points up the capacity of all human beings for freedom, acceptance and love within the world, precisely *as human*.[5] 'Whoever wholly accepts his being human . . . has accepted the Son of Man, because in him God accepted man.'[6]

---

(1)   *Documents of Vatican II The Church in the Modern World* para. 22 (GS)
(2)   RUDOLPH BULTMANN *Glauben und Verstehen III* (Tubingen 1962) p. 29
(3)   HUBERT HALBFAS *Theory of Catechetics* (Herder & Herder, 1971) p. 162
(4)   ANDREW GREELEY *The Great Mysteries* (Gill & Macmillan, 1977) p. 59
(5)   Cf. JOHN PAUL II (Unesco courier June 1980) 'I say to you . . . . Behold the man! I wish to proclaim my admiration for the rich creativity of the human mind, for its untiring efforts to fathom and affirm *the identity of man*, of that man who is always present in every form of culture.'
(6)   KARL RAHNER *Theological Investigations IV* (Darton, Longman & Todd, 1974) p. 154

The Risen Christ, the Spirit of Humanity

'. . . Man must be viewed as a distinctive and autonomous value, as bearing in himself the transcendence of personality, with all that ultimately implies. *Man must be affirmed for his own sake*, and not for any other motive or reason: solely for himself! More than this, man must be loved because he is man, love is due to man by virtue of the special dignity which is his. All these affirmations concerning man lie in the very substance of the message of Christ and the mission of the Church.'[7] All that is true of Christ is incipient in us also. Paul acclaims: 'The Spirit of God has made his home in you. If Christ is in you, then your spirit is life itself.' The whole of mankind is destined to be the New Adam, not in a purely spiritual or transcendent sense, but incorporating, as Teilhard de Chardin saw it, the totality of matter, creation and culture, the value of which has been irreversibly emphasised in the Word made flesh. This reality of God made man, participating completely in his creation, is affirmed in the Christian tradition from earliest times. It was only when our theological thinking began to operate with time-bound Aristotelian categories, and there developed a school of mysticism founded on 'contemptus mundi', that our vision of living experience and the implications of Jesus Christ for the full humanity of each and every one of us, became blurred and distorted. However, the vision has never entirely been lost. Tertullian had no anxieties about it: 'It is in the flesh that salvation hinges.' An eleventh-century saint of the Eastern Church, Simeon, wrote: 'These hands of mine are the hands of God, this body is the body of God through the Incarnation.' Later, St. Teresa made a similar, now famous, affirmation: 'Christ has no body now on earth but yours; no hands but yours; no feet but yours; yours are the eyes through which is to look out Christ's compassion to the world; yours are the feet through which he is to go about doing good; yours are the hands with which he is to bless men now.' In present day Russian liturgy the following statement is to be found:

> 'Everyone who helps another
> is Gethsemane;
> everyone who comforts another
> is the mouth of Christ.'[8]

We are no longer accountable to God in a kind of abstract way. Christ,

---

(7)   JOHN PAUL II, op. cit.
(8)   Cited by DORETHEE SOELLE in *Suffering* (Darton, Longman & Todd, 1975) p. 177

through his cross and resurrection, has shown us what radical humanity is, to be realised not by running away from the world or turning our backs on it in indifference; neither is it to be realised as Maritain warns, by 'imprisoning God in his transcendence.' The way to human fulfilment is to penetrate right to the heart of the world, in all its sufferings, ugliness and desolation as well as its joys, beauty and integrity. In Christ, Küng suggests, our humanity has undergone transfiguration; this is not something tacked on to our human existence, but the revelation of its intrinsic meaning and value. G. Maloney develops this idea. 'Man stands at the centre of the cosmos. Deified man, in whom God lives and through whom he acts to fulfill the world, is the mediator between the disparate and disjointed world and the unity that has been achieved perfectly in the God-Man's humanity through the Incarnation. There can be no transfiguration of the material cosmos except through human beings who themselves by grace have become divinised.'[9] As Christians we can never separate faith in God from faith in man. To do so is a denial of Incarnation, and a refusal of the love made fully manifest in a human being, Jesus Christ. Since he is the pattern of what each person is capable of becoming, a rejection of love incarnate would be tantamount to self-negation; it would in fact be crucifixion.

Salvador Dali's *Christ of St. John of the Cross* is a fine expression of incarnational thinking through the medium of art. By the clever combination of perspectives, Dali synthesises the mundane and the transcendent, man and God. The Cross stretches between heaven and earth, bridging the dark and unknown night of the soul, symbolised by an inky background. The Christ figure is unquestionably human with the tousled hair and contorted hands. Yet the most intriguing feature of the painting is that the viewer sees the composition from two angles simultaneously: we see the fishing-boat and figures at eye-level with the horizon beyond, but we also find ourselves looking down at the world from a point just above the head of Christ — astonishingly, we might say — through the eyes of the Father. Here is an artistic representation of God made man, and we ourselves see it both from the 'horizontal' standpoint of our own concrete humanity and at the same time from the inescapable context of the Spirit within us, constantly transforming our vision of existence. In effect, Dali presents us with a reflection of our own total and unified reality as graced

---

(9)   GEORGE MALONEY, S.J. *Inscape* (Dimension Books, 1978) p. 72

nature. Through the life, death and resurrection of Christ we have the final assurance that the absent God has become Emmanuel, God with us.

> 'In the end, however naked, tall, there is still
> The impossible, possible philosophers' man,
> The man who has had the time to think enough,
> The central man, the human globe, responsive
> As a mirror with a voice, the man of glass,
> Who in a million diamonds sums us up.
> He is the transparence of the place in which
> He is and in his poems we find peace.'[10]

1.4   Grace as Interpersonal Reality

Grace as Context and Capacity

Over the past three decades or so theology has endeavoured to extend the limits of Tridentine thought on the character and meaning of grace. The 'two planes' model, by which the natural plane was constituted as simple facticity, while the supernatural was a 'donum superadditum', badly distorted the full reality of God's life in man. First of all, it was thoroughly extrinsicist in its language and implied an objectivity about the concept of grace which amounted to reification. This was intensified by an over-emphasis on the spatio-temporal imagery employed in the model, namely the dimensions of the vertical and the horizontal. The symbols of language are rich and indispensible and these terms will, of course, always be used as we search for a more or less adequate expression of the Christian faith; but they should never be understood in a static, literal sense. The dangers of limiting our understanding of grace in this way are strikingly reflected in the way we have interpreted the sacraments until quite recently. (Cf Ch.1 6) Here we have seen that an undue preoccupation with the 'reception' of grace as an individual possession has been at the expense of its universal and interpersonal character. Attitudes of exclusivism tended to overlook the wider communitarian implications, and grace became on the whole a very private affair between the individual and God. Reinhold Niebuhr suggests that in this way 'grace mediated through the security of parental affection, or the self-forgetfulness prompted by a crisis or the pull

---

(10)   WALLACE STEVENS *Asides on the Oboe*; cited by CORNELIUS ERNST in *Multiple Echo* (Darton, Longman & Todd, 1979) p. 12

of the exercise of creative capacities or of responsibilities and loyalties to a cause greater than the self, all of which are the daily experiences of mankind, are minimised in favour of a 'saving grace' mediated by the church and consciously sought by the believer.'[1]

Present day interpretations have changed for a number of reasons: the biblical and patristic renewal; studies in the psychological factors involved in faith; new and growing movements of thought within Christianity; the penetration of secularisation into various areas of human life. Prior to Vatican II it came gradually to be recognised that the privacy of grace was not a necessary presupposition to maintain the principle of its gratuitousness. Notable contributors towards the rediscovery of the vitality of grace were Joseph Marechal, Henri de Lubac and Yves Congar. Rahner's thinking derives much from these thinkers and the Council took up a good deal of the renewed approach in its documents. The reality of grace is seen to be multidimensional, encompassing ontological, psychological and social aspects of man's being. Moreover, this reality is shown as truly Incarnational in that it is present to *all* men as the fundamental motivator of love, the ultimate condition of all goodness in the world. '. . . Linked with the paschal mystery and patterned on the dying Christ, (the Christian) will hasten forward to resurrection in the strength which comes from hope. All this holds true not only for Christians but for all men of goodwill in whose hearts grace works in an unseen way. For, since Christ died for all men, and since the ultimate vocation of mankind is in fact one and divine, we ought to believe that the Holy Spirit in a manner known only to God offers to every man the possiblity of being associated with this paschal mystery.'[2]

We must recover still more, however, an awareness of human potentialities in our theology of grace, for only by so doing can we establish the real value of the Incarnation and thereby release God from his transcendence. Otherwise the tendency is for God to remain a rather decorative figure, with little credible impact on living human existence. We must rediscover man, suggested Maritain, if we are to rediscover God. Man is graced from the moment of creation. By constitution he is, as Moran puts it, 'freedom for God', existing by 'the breath of life which that same God has breathed into him. There is more than 'a sense and taste for the infinite'

---

(1)   REINHOLD NIEBUHR *Man's Nature and His Communities* (New York, 1965), p. 119
(2)   Vatican II, op. cit. para. 22

about man; he and his whole world have been taken hold of and continue to be by the power of God's Spirit. Grace, therefore, does not designate a 'supernatural' area standing above and beyond created nature, it 'refers instead to that significant ground of all being which circumscribes and supports the horizon and depth of all everyday experience.'[3] The liturgy is rich with expressions of this truth; God is the fountain, the source of all creation, 'all life, all holiness comes from you.'[4] Grace is the innate capability each man possesses to relate, forgive, overcome suffering, create, invent, imagine, explore — indeed to do anything which is a positive option for love and growth. Not only is it the *capacity* to do these things, it is the transformation brought about in any life-situation by the actualisation of that capacity. Grace is the context, capacity and transformation bound up in every moment of love and authentic self-realisation. 'However much we emphasise that grace remains the supre...e surprise for our nature, we have to affirm with equal force that grace sets our deepest humanity free, precisely because it restores our most authentic humanity to us and by this means *humanises* us to an eminent degree. . . . Properly speaking we do not receive grace; we do not possess it as something foreign to us, or as something entering into us from outside; but *we are our grace*.'[5] As Caesar wisely observes in Thornton Wilder's *The Ides of March*: 'I seem to have known all my life, but to have refused to acknowledge, that all, all love is one, and that the very mind with which I ask these questions is awakened, sustained and instructed only by love.'[6]

Grace as Gift Between Persons
Jesus is the perfected pattern of graced humanity. The ultimate condition of our existence is fully actualised in him through a life and death of unfailing love. But this love was not a flimsy abstract kind of love, neither was it a private business between Jesus and the Father. Scripture is full of the outreaching of love — to publicans, prostitutes, prisoners, tax-collectors, the handicapped, diseased and poverty-stricken. There is nothing privileged or comfortable about the love of Jesus; it is radically communitarian and

(3)   HALBFAS op. cit. p.158
(4)   Eucharistic Prayer III
(5)   PIET FRANSEN *Divine Grace and Man* (Mentor-Omega, 1965), pp. 173–4
(6)   THORNTON WILDER *The Ides of March*, quoted in Bozzo, Theological Studies (as below).

constantly realises itself in concern for others. For grace is a gift that demands to be incarnated in human experience. 'If grace means essentially God's gift of himself to man,' observes Edward Bozzo, 'if the divine nature manifests itself in no other way than through human nature, if the logical consequence of the Incarnation is that man is for man the way to God, then grace can be nothing else but communal in its drive.'[7] The energies of the Resurrection cannot remain locked in a single human heart, they must be communicated between persons, for as the Council asserts, 'man . . . cannot fully find himself except through a sincere gift of himself.'[8] 'By his innermost nature man is a social being, and unless he relates himself to others he can neither live nor develop his potential.'[9] Love that is not active and outgoing evacuates the meaning of grace and the true vocation of man, for we need others in order to be most fully ourselves. 'Love alone is capable of uniting living beings in such a way as to complete and fulfil them, for it alone takes them and joins them by what is deepest in themselves. This is a fact of daily experience.'[10]

> 'If you want to be free of yourself
> you must build a bridge over the gulf
> of loneliness your selfishness
> has found, and look beyond.
> Listen to another,
> and especially,
> try loving him or her,
> and not just "me".'[11]

Revelation 'does not find us located in the rarefied regions of a stratospheric spirituality,' Fransen insists, where the real issues and responsibilities of this world are lost sight of; God speaks to us in the actual concrete situations of our personal existence, transforming them and giving them their deepest significance. Paul reminds us that the living out of a graced humanity entails 'filling your minds with everything that is true, everything that is noble, everything that is good and pure, everything that we love and honour, and everything that can be thought virtuous or

---

(7) EDWARD BOZZO *The Neglected Dimension: Grace in Interpersonal Context* (Theological Studies Vol. 29. No. 3, 1968). p. 504.
(8) Vatican II, op. cit. para. 24
(9) Ibid. para. 12
(10) TEILHARD De CHARDIN *The Phenomenon of Man* (Fontana, 1974) p. 292
(11) HELDER CAMARA *The Desert is Fertile* (Sheed & Ward, 1974) pp. 16–17

worthy of praise.' We must be imitators of God by walking in love, for without love nothing can be gained either in terms of individual growth or community development. Grace is the dimension of the profundity and sacredness of all reality; it is the living presence of love and value in our experience of the world, and it is ours to actualise or deny in our freedom. In all our relationships, decisions and enterprises — whether joyful or sorrowful — grace is the gratuitous condition, the context and the quality of love-in-community which constitutes the fullness of human existence.

Hermann Hesse's novel *Siddhartha* contains some of the most evocative passages in recent literature. In one of these passages which describes the remarkable experience of a disciple at the deathbed of the Master, our understanding of the inevitability and universality of the grace of Christ is deepened and clarified. 'He no longer saw the face of his friend Siddhartha. Instead he saw other faces, many faces, a long series, a continuous stream of faces — hundreds, thousands which all came and disappeared and yet all seemed to be there at the same time, which all continually changed and renewed themselves and which were yet all Siddhartha. He saw the face of a fish, of a carp, with tremendous painfully opened mouth, a dying fish with dimmed eyes. He saw the face of a newly born child, red and full of wrinkles, ready to cry. He saw the face of a murderer, saw him plunge a knife into the body of a man; at the same moment he saw this criminal kneeling down, bound, and his head cut off by an executioner. He saw the naked bodies of men and women in the postures and transports of passionate love. He saw corpses stretched out, still, cold, empty. He saw the heads of animals — boars, crocodiles, elephants, oxen, birds. He saw all these forms and faces in a thousand relationships to each other, all helping each other, loving, hating and destroying each other and becoming newly born. . . . Govinda bowed low, right down to the ground, in front of the man sitting there motionless, whose smile reminded him of everything that he had ever loved in his life, of everything that had ever been of value and holy in his life.'[12] Grace is indeed this 'smile of unity over the flowing forms' of man's experience of life.

---

(12)   HERMANN HESSE *Siddhartha* (Bantam, 1974) pp. 150–152

1.5   The Church as Sign-Community of the True World

The Church for the World

The history of ecclesiology represents Christianity's attempt to maintain, in line with the reality of the Incarnation, the necessary tension between the visible, concrete historical aspect of the Church and its character as spiritual, eschatological communion. The Church came into being as the community of those who witnessed to the Resurrection. In the early Christian era this experience of the Spirit of the Risen Christ was vivid and immediate and far less structured than it later became. Men and women presented the evidence for the continued presence of Christ, not so much in formulations as in the quality of their own lives: in joy and hope they built a community of love and trust. 'By this, we know that we have passed from death to life, by the love we have for each other.' (1 John 3: 14) With the passage of time and the pressures of increased membership, the Church's self-understanding became more structured and governed more by organisational factors. It was only after several centuries of a predominantly institutional understanding of the Church that the emphasis shifted once more to greater openness and flexibility in ecclesiology, culminating in the Second Vatican Council. This shift of emphasis is perhaps rooted in two main areas of development in recent years. First, the recovery of a more existential understanding of grace which has unavoidably influenced sacramental theology. Second, the Christian view of the relationship between the Church and the world has undergone considerable renewal, partly as a result of modern secularisation and partly in consequence of a real recognition of the eschatological significance of history.

The world is the graced arena in which man strives always to become more and more truly human. It is the history within which God became incarnate and established forever its essential value. In Christ God accepted the world definitively, so that everything in it was shown to be decisive for the salvation of man. 'The Spirit of God gives life to all things: "you send forth your spirit and they are created": birds of the air, beasts of the field, fish in the sea, and man. All that lives, lives in virtue of the power of God, all have the spirit of God.'[1] Nevertheless the decisive nature of the created world must be actualised by man himself in the process of history. All his activities — discovery, invention, technology, artistic creativity — should be

---

(1)   LEONARD JOHNSTON *The Flesh and the Spirit* (The Way Vol. 11/2, 1971) p. 98

positively directed towards deeper humanisation, for through Incarnation the world has become man's dearest responsibility. In this process, secularisation, which sometimes seems to be a world-construction devoid of God, is not necessarily a de-christianising of history, but rather represents its liberation to become the context for man's realisation of salvation. 'The secularity of the world,' claims Metz, 'should not reveal itself to us primarily as a dethroning of Christ within the world in an historically intensified protest against him, but as the decisive point of his dominion in history. . . . Grace is freedom; it bestows upon things the scarcely measured depths of their own being. It calls things out of all their sinful alienation into their own. It calls the world into its perfect worldliness.'[2]

Only in the light of the world's significance can the sacramental character of the Church community be identified. It can never constitute a privileged elite within the world, for the reality to which the ecclesial community is witness is a universal one, embracing the dimensions of humanity itself. 'There is only one God,' said Irenaeus, 'there is only one Son who carries out the will of the Father. And there is only one human race in which God's mysterious designs are brought to fulfilment.' Consequently, the visible Church exists in function of humanity; the movements and conflicts of the world – the signs of the times – are the Church's responsibility insofar as it must endeavour constantly to show forth the centrality of love in human existence. 'Christ entered the world's history as a perfect man, taking that history up into himself and summarising it. He himself revealed to us that "God is love". At the same time he taught us that the new command of love was the basic law of human perfection and hence of the world's transformation.'[3] Therefore, 'by her relationship with Christ, the Church is a kind of sacrament of intimate union with God, and of the unity of all mankind.'[4] In short, the Church is the sign-community, the community of awareness that God has already placed in the hearts of men the real possibility of becoming other Christs. In Origen's words: 'Our Lord Jesus Christ, the word of God, of his boundless love, became what we are that he might make us what he himself is.' Thus, the task of the sign-community is continually to highlight and celebrate the presence of the Spirit everywhere, to announce that Incarnation has happened and

(2)   J. B. METZ *The Theology of the World* (Buns & Oates, 1969), pp. 19, 49
(3)   Vatican II op. cit. para. 38
(4)   Vatican II Documents, *The Dogmatic Constitution in the Church* para. 1

corporately to express its full implications and meaning for every human being. (Cf. Fig. 2)

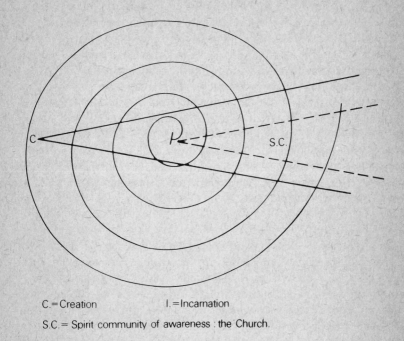

C.=Creation   I.=Incarnation

S.C.= Spirit community of awareness : the Church.

Figure 2: The Church as Sign-community of the True World

'Christians cannot boast that they have themselves an excellent way of life for they have little to point to when they boast. They only confess — we were blind in our distrust of being, now we begin to see; we were aliens and alienated in a strange empty world, now we begin sometimes to feel at home; we were in love with ourselves and all our little cities, now we are falling in love, we think, with being itself, with the city of God, the universal community of which God is the source and governor. And for all this we are indebted to Jesus Christ, in our history, and in that depth of the spirit in which we grope with our theologies and theories of symbols.'[5]

(5)   H. RICHARD NIEBUHR *The Responsible Self; An Essay in Moral Philosophy* (New York: Harper & Row, 1963) p. 178

The Church must *affirm* the world within which it moves, insofar as the world's enterprises tend towards humanisation. Conversely, wherever men's actions tend to damage and do violence to the love that is ever-present, then the Church must function as *protest* against such regression and alienation. Always, the ecclesial community, the specific Church, must serve the needs of humanity by helping the realities of the world to find the true and authentic source of their own being, and by reflecting in its own activities the quality of love that it seeks to signify. 'The essential nature of the Church, therefore, is to be this mystery of love, of the divine love revealing itself and communicating itself to men. All the sign-language of doctrine and ritual has no purpose but to reveal and communicate this love. This is the light in which the doctrine, the ritual and the organisation of the Church are to be judged. . . . The Kingdom of God, the reign of the Spirit, has to take shape in this world. . . . (The Church) has continually to renew itself, . . . to discover again its original message, to define it in the light of the present day, to manifest its power to transform men's lives.'[6]

The Trinity as Model of a Loving Community

Nowadays, the doctrine of the Trinity often appears to be a needless complication of our idea of God. We have in the past either struggled valiantly with the metaphysical concept of 'three persons in one,' or relegated the doctrine to the realm of unapproachable mystery, food for the academic theologians with very little relevance to Christian living. The Incarnational approach maintains that obscurity results when we seek the meaning of the Trinity in areas too far removed from ourselves, remote from actual human experience. We must give to doctrines the flesh and blood that bestows upon them their real value, for if they are developing expressions of God's revelation in Christ, then they are necessarily statements about man himself and his own understanding of the world.

The Trinity casts light on man's existence specifically because it is about true community and its unfolding realisation within the history of man. It focuses for us the recapitulation in Christ of the whole world since the moment of creation, and it points us towards the future hope of perfected human community. The early Christians, after Pentecost, experienced so vividly the presence of the Spirit of Christ as the personal and

---

(6)   BEDE GRIFFITHS *Return to the Centre* (Collins, 1976) pp. 117–118

dynamic force building up and strengthening the community, that they began gradually to understand God's plan as he had intended it from the beginning. As Jews they were totally committed to the action of God as Creator, as the Father, the divine impetus of all creation. The Old Testament contains profound expressions of this reality. 'Thou art clothed with honour and majesty, who coverest thyself with light as with a garment, who has stretched out the heavens like a tent, who hast laid the beams of thy chambers on the waters, who makest the clouds thy chariot, who ridest on the wings of the wind. . . . Thou hast made the moon to mark the seasons; the sun to know its time for setting. Thou makest darkness and it is night, when all the beasts of the forest creep forth.' (Psalm 104) Then the Christ, the promised Messiah, arrived. He lived as a man amongst men, loving, suffering and dying. But he overcame death and in so doing transcended his own particularity by extending to all men the enabling gift of his Spirit, by which we too are capable of going beyond ourselves. In the overwhelming experience of resurrection, the community realised intensely that the Spirit of the Risen Christ continued in their midst, that this love was really present and incarnated in community wherever people loved and related. 'Important as the person of Jesus Christ is in the story of the Gospel, the magitude of the event of revelation is obscured if one does not see that a significant dimension of that event was the energy of the spirit that broke afresh from the community of people into which this new life had come. They were transformed, the Gospels say — yes, but not just individually; relationally as well. Centres of an innovating righteousness appeared within the culture, in which the New Creation became flesh again and again. The Christian witness becomes vivid and impressive when it is seen in its corporate context. The new life . . . becomes an enduring depth of grace within the relationships that body forth the living Christ and his reconciling Word, in the decisions, acts, negotiations, and responses of men and women working at pertinent issues in society. . . . Here we have the seminal beginnings of the Church as a witnessing community becoming the body of Christ.'[7]

Thus, the Trinity expresses the truth that God is personal and loving; that he is in fact not an abstraction or a totally transcendent entity, but a God radically involved in history and creation; that in all his movements he is eternally vital and irrevocably incarnate. He is love's initiative and

---

(7)   BERNARD E. MELAND *The Realities of Faith* (New York: Oxford University Press 1962) p. 261

love's response, and he is the permanent and immanent gift to man by which each member of the human race himself becomes Trinitarian, that is, capable of loving and being loved with unlimited openness and freedom. 'God is love,' said Augustine, 'the very same love with which we love.'

Since the Church is the sign-community of the spiritual depth and height of human existence, the doctrine of the Trinity is indispensable to our understanding of it, for this doctrine is *the* model of loving community. Instead of searching for the meaning of the Trinity in an ontology centred on an objective and removed God, we should seek it in the universal and incarnational sphere of interpersonal communication actually present in our experience of life. Through the action of God in Christ every man is set free to call forth the creativity of love in others. As the community of those who are conscious of it, the Church should seek to illuminate and intensify this creativity by deepening its own Trinitarian character and encouraging the growth of genuine and loving community in the whole family of man.

1.6   The Sacraments as Celebrations of a New Humanity

The world is too old now and too wise to find satisfaction in definition of sacraments which conjure up pictures of channels, pipelines and injections of grace which protect people from contamination in a bad, threatening world. In the theology and teaching of the sacraments, phrases about renewing the inner dynamo of the soul, charging the spiritual batteries, refuelling the grace-tank for the dangerous journey of life may have been well meant but in reality they are based on a very questionable undertanding of 'the natural' and 'the supernatural.' The sacraments and their graces are not extra additions placed on top of, or alongside, ordinary life like divine icing on a human cake. An understanding of the sacraments begins, as we have already observed, with the world itself and with the basic truth of faith that what we call sanctifying grace and the divine life is present everywhere (cf. Ch. 1.1 & 1.2). The one exception is where a man deliberately says 'no' to this vision and truth about life revealed through the Incarnation (cf. Ch. 1.8).

All Creation Holy
Already we have discussed how by virtue of creation and still more of the

Incarnation nothing here below is profane for the Christian. The first step towards a deeper understanding of sacraments is to see them in the context of a world already permeated and filled with God's presence. In the very person of Christ himself, God and man, this inter-penetration has taken place. The human is now the locus of the divine. The redemption has happened. The Holy Spirit is in men. The art is to help men become what they are. To the analytical mind sacramental grace is a complicated phenomenon which needs many terms and treatises. To the saint it is a simple, rich and enriching experience bringing the kind of knowing that surpasses all knowledge. Grace is life fully lived. God's basic gift to men is the lives they live and the good earth from which they make their living. In the *Furrow* James Mackey writes 'The life which is now being called God's primordial and perennial grace to man is precisely the life of everyman's everyday experience. It is man's working and eating, walking in the fields or on the seashore, playing for his team or dancing in his club, sleeping with his wife or talking with his friends, suffering the slings and arrows of outrageous fortune or holding out a helping hand to his fellow man, deciding what is best with the best guidance he can get and getting up for Mass on Sundays. All that is grace.'[1]

Christopher Kiesling explains why this is so. 'Christian faith is born of the experience of Jesus Christ, a man who was born, lived, suffered, and died like other men, yet in whom God was reconciling all things to himself. Through Jesus Christ men were given the insight that in ordinary human existence, its joys and sorrows, its hopes and disappointments, its daily activities like eating and relaxing, conversing and enjoying companionship, its use of things and interaction with people, God is at work transforming men into his children in whom he wishes to dwell in a communion of life.'[2]

The Vatican Council's document *The Church in the Modern World* makes it clear that in the past we over-emphasized the notion of two distinct worlds, one sacred and one profane. Gergory Baum, who was a 'peritus' at the Council, expresses this insight as few others can: 'The radical distinction between the sacred and the profane has been overcome in the person of Christ. In Christ it is revealed that the locus of the divine is the human. In him it is made manifest that God speaks in and through the words and gestures of men. The Christian way of worship, therefore,

---

(1)   MACKEY, J. *Grace* (article in *The Furrow*, Vol. XXIV. No. 6: 1973) p. 341
(2)   KIESLING, C. *Paradigms of Sacramentality*: (article in *Worship*, Vol. 44: No. 7: 1970) p. 426

can no longer consist in sacred rites by which men are severed from the ordinary circumstances of their lives. Christian liturgy is, rather, the celebration of the deepest dimension of human life, which is God's self-communication to men. Liturgy unites men more closely to their daily lives. Worship remembers and celebrates the marvellous things God works in the lives of men, purifies and intensifies these gifts, makes men more sensitive to the Word and Spirit present in their secular lives. The sacraments of Christ enable men to celebrate the deepest dimension of their lives, namely God's gift of himself, in a way that renders the dimension more powerful.'[3]

The Church as Sacrament

This hidden involvement of God in the humanization of man has become fully, definitively and unconditionally manifest in Jesus Christ, the Word made flesh and it is this Christ that is proclaimed and celebrated in the Church. In the Church we have not only the source of salvation for those who belong to it, we see also in the Church God's redemptive plan for the entire world of men. In the Church is proclaimed and celebrated the mystery of redemption from within that summons man everywhere. E. Schillebeeck writes in *The Church Today*, 'What the Church has to offer us explicity is already implicitly present in human life as a whole; it is the mystery of salvation. The Church reveals, proclaims, and celebrates in thankfulness the deepest dimension of that which is being fulfilled in the world. . . . The Church is in fact the world where the world has come fully to itself, where the world confesses and acknowledges the deepest mystery of its own life, the mystery of salvation fulfilled through Christ.'[4]

Unless we are aware of the sacramental nature of all reality and of the fact that our whole Christian life is worship we cannot fully appreciate the constantly revealing mystery of the Incarnation, of the Church and of the sacraments. There is a unity and a synthesis being sought for in today's interpretation of the Faith that gives resonance and clarity to what, for many, has up to now been a collection of disconnected statements that defied a certain level of investigation because they were said to be concerned with mysteries and therefore totally impenetrable by mere human

---

(3)   BAUM, G. Man Becoming (op. cit.) pp. 75 & 76
(4)   SCHILLEBEECKX, E. *Christian Faith and the Future of the World*: essay in *The Church Today*, p. 82 & quoted in BAUM (op. cit.) p. 63

minds. Now that 'mystery' is seen in the light of the truth which is the necessary condition of all human knowing, there is a realization by the Church of the obligation to continue searching for a deeper understanding of the God in whose image we are made. What has been said up to now is that the world and all it contains comes from God. The breath-taking mystery of creation, life and the universe, past and present, is an incredibly beautiful sign of love, communicated to men, and reflecting the wisdom and loveliness of God. This in itself makes the world already holy and sacred. And then, this presence of the Spirit and the Word which was there in creation in and from the beginning, as St. John reminds us, is fleshed in Jesus Christ, consecrating again from within a nature and an earthly reality that was sorely in need of salvation. We then saw that this Church was the stretching into time of this mystery of incarnation and redemption, the continuing presence in the world of a Christian community who possess a faith-vision of human existence, who believe that the Gospel is God's good news that humanity is possible, that community can work and that the impossible may be possible after all. 'Make ready for Christ,' writes Thomas Merton, 'whose smile, like lightning, sets free the song of everlasting glory that now sleeps, in your paper flesh, like dynamite.' And finally we see the sacraments themselves as privileged moments in the process of encounter between God and man. They are not there merely to give us the extra willpower to keep in line with the law, or to provide a pattern of uniformity for 'practising.' Whether we describe them as personal encounters with Christ, or the fullest moments of the Church's life, the sacraments basically take the earthly realities of our human existence, birth, reconciliation, sickness, love, and to the eyes of faith they show forth the deeper meaning hidden within, the silent activity of the Spirit, gradually sanctifying and redeeming every aspect of daily life until the time when God will be 'all in all.' 'That which is lived out in an everyday manner outside the sacraments grows to its full maturity in them. The anonymity of everyday Christian living is removed by the telling power of Christ's symbolic action in and through his Church. Therefore, the sacraments cannot be isolated from the organic unity of a whole persevering Christian life.'[5]

---

(5)   SCHILLEBEECKX, E. *Christ the Sacrament* (Sheed and Ward: 1963) pp. 246 & 247

Sacraments and Meaning

In *Doctrine and Life*[6] Sean Fagan explains that Francis of Assisi, with his eyes of faith, had no difficulty with this kind of vision. For him the sun and the moon, fire and water, animals and humans, all spoke of God. The smallest particle of creation was a theophany, a revelation of God. As Christians we all ought to have this kind of vision. All too often the Christian's act of seeing is a mere seeing which stops at appearances and does not go on to the meaning. He needs eyes to read the wind, the stars, people's hands and faces, in such a way that he sees more than what appears.
But there are moments which stand out from all the others, moments which come like a gift, moments 'when the focus shifts and a single leaf becomes a universe, a rock speaks prophecies and a smile transforms a relationship.' We call such moments sacred, because in them we glimpse something of the sacredness of life, the wonder of God. Following on from this 'what needs to be emphasized is that the sacraments become more meaningful when they are seen as high points, peak moments, special occasions in a life that is already sacramental in its own right. They are of a piece with the rest of life and reality, not irruptions from a different world. In this sense it is more helpful to approach them from the context of life as a whole. They are moments of insight, bringing home to us, each in its own way, the deeper meaning of our life and destiny. The sacraments declare forth what is otherwise hidden in the darkness of the world, in the routine of everyday life. They bring into focus and draw our attention to what we tend to ignore and lose sight of when we are busy about many things.'[7]

In time and space, in ordinary signs and symbols, the scattered fragments of our lives are gathered up and for a moment given meaning in the light of Christ. John Macquarrie writes 'In the word and sacraments, the divine presence is focussed so as to communicate itself to us with a directness and intensity like that of the incarnation itself. . . .'[8]

Paradigms of Sacramentality

The sacraments are the personal acts of the Risen Christ, visible signs that

---

(6)   FAGAN, S. *Sacraments in the Spiritual Life* (article in *Doctrine & Life*, Vol. 23, No. 8: 1973) p. 40
(7)   FAGAN, S. (op. cit.) p. 42
(8)   MACQUARRIE, J. *Principles of Christian Theology* (S.C.M. Press 1966) p. 398

God personally concerns himself with human life, with our concrete fleshly existence, especially at those decisive moments in which something above and beyond man is at stake, birth, growth, the shared meal, marriage, illness, death. There is no magic here, no short-cuts to sanctity, no slot-machine cheap grace.

Referring to someone who comes to celebrate the Eucharist, K. Rahner writes, 'He offers up the world under the form of bread and wine, knowing that the world is already constantly offering itself up to the incomprehensible God under its own forms, in the ecstasy of its joy and the bitterness of its sorrow. He looks, praising, at God's ineffable light, knowing that this vision takes place most radically where eyes weep tears of blood, or glass over as they see the approach of death. He knows that he is proclaiming the death of the Lord, in as much as this death, once died, lives on always in the world, is built into the inmost centre of the world, and is truly enacted again in that man, who, whether he knows this expressly or not, 'dies in the Lord.' He knows that he is proclaiming at Mass the Coming of the Lord, because the Lord is *already realizing* his coming in the world in everything that drives the world on towards its goal. He receives under holy signs the true Body of the Lord, knowing this to be worthless, were he not to communicate with *that* Body of God which is the world itself and its fate: he partakes of the one *Body* so as to remain always in communion with that other body in the reality of his life.'[9]

Working within the same understanding of sacramentality, Tad Guzie suggests that it is not baptism that makes us members of God's family. 'We belong to God's family from the first moment of our existence. Christian faith and baptism are a response to a call to belong *in a particular way* to the family of God. Through baptism we are initiated into the family of Jesus, into a community which is called to become *aware* of how the love of God has been made manifest in Jesus. To be baptized is not to enter the world of grace, because the grace and love of God is already there, it is freely given, it surrounds our existence, and we are all in contact with it from the first moment of our conception. But to be initiated into the family of Jesus is a different matter, a matter of entering into a conscious process in which the business of dying and rising becomes the pattern for one's life-style.'[10]

(9)   RAHNER, K. *Secular Life and the Sacraments (II)* (article in *The Tablet*, Vol. 225, No. 6823: 1971) p. 267
(10)   GUZIE, T. *Theological Challenges*: (article in A symposium on Christian Initiation, W. Reedy (ed.) Sadlier Press: 1979) pp. 168 & 169

Referring to the sacrament of Penance he asks, 'Do we begin with the mystery of God's love, or are we to remain fixated with sin and evil? God's continual and faithful love for us is *the* "good news". We are never not forgiven. The problem is our acceptance of the forgiveness that is always there for us.

The question is not of becoming 'okay with God', but rather of receiving and celebrating the love that surrounds us from the first moment of our existence. The sacraments do not confer a grace that was absent. Sacraments proclaim and enable us to own a love that is already present to us. A sacrament celebrates the Lord's giving, certainly. But his giving is not confined to the sacrament. What we need to focus on within the sacrament, is our taking the love of God home with us, with a fresh awareness of that love. And that new awareness is the substantial part of the "grace of the sacrament".[11]

We leave the last word in this section to Kiesling. 'Baptism as incorporation into the Christian community is a paradigm of the sacramentality of all entrance into human community: family, city, nation, labour union, political party, school, bridge club. Confirmation is a model of all commitment to worthy human associations, causes, and ideals. Penance is paradigmatic of all human reconciliation, whether between members of families or of other communities, between proponents of opposing ideas of government, between nations at rivalry.

Further, anointing the sick is paradigmatic of the sacramentality of all care of the bodily and mentally ill, the economically and culturally deprived, the down trodden, the rejected. Ordination is paradigmatic of the sacramentality of all human responsibility for the welfare of others, especially their common welfare, of all human leadership and government, whether in the narrow circle of the family or the wide circle of international life. The eucharist is paradigmatic of the sacramentality of all self-sacrifice for others and for the causes of justice, love, freedom, and truth. It is paradigmatic of the sacramentality of every meal which men share and of all human sharing, whether economic, cultural or spiritual. Marriage is paradigmatic of the sacramentality of every human encounter, every human friendship, every human love. It is paradigmatic also of the banalities of daily social life of every kind. The word of God (in the sense of the Bible, the oral traditions behind it, and the words of God's spokesmen behind

---

(11)   Ibid. pp. 172 & 173

them) may be added to this list as paradigmatic of the sacramentality of all human speech and communication.'[12]

1.7   The Eucharist as the Real Presence of Love in Creation

The Communitarian Meaning of the Eucharistic Symbols

One of the most urgent tasks facing a truly sacramental Church is the recovery of its proper eucharistic character. The somewhat formal and stylised liturgy with which most of us are familiar frequently seems to conceal rather than reveal the full implications of Eucharist for human living. As with the other sacraments we have often fallen into the trap of 'privatising' the Eucharist, of seeing the reception of Holy Communion as a pipeline of grace. A history of magical attitudes towards the host has served to reinforce this, and the essential question of what do these symbols of bread and wine *mean* for man, is subordinated to a preoccupation with what is happening *out there* on the altar. This problem of overcoming a static, individualistic and non-existential form of thinking is the very same that haunts all the various areas of theology we are considering.

Most theologians today are agreed that whether Jesus and his disciples were sharing a ritual fellowship meal or celebrating the annual Passover, he was not as such doing anything at the Last Supper which would have been an innovation in the life of any good Jew. 'As often as you do this, do it in memory of me.' Surely the most significant words are not so much 'do this' but 'in memory of me.' After the resurrection, in the powerful experience of fellowship and community, the disciples indeed realised that Jesus had given to the breaking of bread a new and universal meaning – not just in terms of a passover meal, but in relation to all meals shared in companionship and every situaion of self-giving, 'Whenever two or three are gathered together in my name, there am I in their midst.' Moreover, the solidarity and unity created by eating in common, is one of the most profound factors in the communitarian movement of the world. Food and drink have the capacity to consolidate human relationships. Accustomed as we are on the one hand to snatching a quick bite before rushing for a train, and on the other hand to the ill-effects of overeating and excessive drinking, we have to an extent lost our sensitivity towards meals in the modern western world. Nevertheless, the sharing of what food we do have whether it be the child's

---

(12)   KIESLING, C. (op. cit.) p. 427

apple or the executive's banquet, is the crucial point. For all food is the food of life; all bread in a real sense is the bread of life. It cannot be denied that our capacity to share or deprive, to accept or reject, create or destroy, is the making or the breaking of other people — this is true at all levels of our life. For this reason the sacramental Church, which points up the spiritual quality of the world and signals the decisiveness of men's relationships, carries a special responsibility. 'If the Eucharist is *lived* by those who celebrate it, sharing will have to be practised by them. This is a primary requisite of the eucharist community or church. Since love is for all, sharing must also be with all others too. The Eucahrist is anti-individualistic.'[1]

For those who might argue that coke and crisps would do equally well in the celebration of Eucharist, bread and wine are not simply random symbols. Bread 'which earth has given and human hands have made' is the symbol of our own becoming and of our communion with all mankind, in creativity and joy as well as toil, deprivation and suffering. Wine, 'fruit of the vine and work of human hands,' symbolises newness of being, man re-created in all his capacities to liberate, heal and sustain as well as to crush and alienate. As soon as we attempt to separate these symbols from the revelatory meaning they carry for human existence, then we lose sight of true Eucharist, for it is in the integration of symbol and life that Christian love and its expression take on flesh and blood. Eucharist is primarily an *event*, involving the interrelationship of people in both a local and a global context. If, in our liturgical celebration of Eucharist, we analyse the symbols and the living community as independent components with separable meanings then the intrinsic correspondence between the love which Eucharist signifies and the responsibility of the Christian community in the world is lost. Eucharist becomes a cult, just one more ritual with too little relevance. 'If *we* have lost our revelation about love and meaning, then we are no use to the world at all. But if we can rediscover it, then we are at one with Christ, at one with the Suffering Servant, in building up the old wastes, raising up the former desolations, repairing the waste cities, the desolations of many generations. Like the Suffering Servant we shall be permitted to bind up the broken-hearted, to proclaim liberty to the captives and the opening of the prison to them that are bound, to proclaim the acceptable year of the Lord.'[2]

---

(1) TISSA BALASURIYA *The Eucharist and Human Liberation* (Orbis, 1979) p. 81

(2) MONICA FURLONG *With Love to the Church* (Hodder & Stroughton, 1965) pp. 94–5

The Incarnational Basis of Eucharistic Celebration

In the same way that the Church exists for the sake of the true world, its liturgical celebration throws into relief the real presence of love in creation. The sacramental breaking of bread derives from and celebrates the wider spectrum of human experiences. Within the reality of Incarnation all such experiences are potentially redemptive: family life, friendship, work, study, leisure activities and every other dimension of our existence in the world. In the sweat of the labourer, the routine of the factory-worker, the tears of a child, the grief of the bereaved, the commitment of a parent, the joy of a friend and the blood of the soldier, is the living mystery of Easter.

'Now my friends, now I will tell you what belongs to God. *You* belong to God. You do not *belong* to Caesar. You belong to God. What does that mean? It means that you belong to yourself. And it means that you belong to each other. You are all free. But you do not know that you are free. Come closer. . . I will tell you things kept secret since the world began. Do you know what it is to be a man? Come. Dare to listen and I will tell you how to change the world. . . . . A light must be lit. The world need not always be in darkness. The world need not always be filled with the hungry. . . . There are better things than have yet been seen. I will show you.'[3]

Since the Paschal mystery is really present in every attempt to relate, to share, to discover, to create, and to grow in community, then the human predicament itself is the central dynamism for specifically ecclesial celebration in sacrament and liturgy. Conscious of what has been achieved and revealed in Christ's death and resurrection, the Church must carry its Eucharist on to the table of the world, and assume responsiblility for the humanisation of creation. It can do no less, 'for the partaking of the Body and Blood of Christ does nothing other than transform us into that which we consume.'[4] The pattern of true loving humanity established in Jesus, is the only paradigm for our actions and attitudes.

'Leave this chanting and singing and telling of beads.
Whom do you worship in this lonely dark corner of the temple
    with all the doors shut?
Open your eyes and see that God is not in front of you.
He is there where the farmer is tilling the hard ground and where
    the labourer is breaking stones.

---

(3)   DENNIS POTTER *Son of Man* (Penguin, 1971) Act II scene 6 pp. 78–79
(4)   Vatican II, The Dogmatic Constitution on the Church, para. 26.

He is with them in the sun and the rain and his garment is covered
  with dust.
Put off your holy cloak and like him come down on to the dusty
  soil.
Deliverance?
Where will you find deliverance?
Our master himself has joyfully taken on the bonds of creation,
  he is bound with us for ever.
Come out of your meditations and leave aside the flowers and the
  incense.
What harm is there if your clothes become tattered and stained?
Meet him and stand by him in the toil and in the sweat of your
  brow.'[5]

Juan Luis Segundo suggests that we must not be 'gospel consumers'
but 'gospel creators'. Perhaps Christians should make continual efforts to
authenticate their sacramental life by being not only 'Eucharist consumers'
but of necessity 'Eucharist creators' too, committed as Christ was to a new
world order in which the basic needs of all humanity are provided for, suffering is alleviated and all the resources of the world shared. Through the
ever more intense presence of love the world is set free and moves towards
its ultimate fulfilment. Among the many masterful representations of the
Last Supper, Salvador Dali's is certainly a very striking one. The almost
transparent quality of the figure of Christ conveys the truth that through
him and in him we see the fullness of created reality and especially of human existence. And not in any ethereal or onesidedly mystical sense. For
the solid torso of a man that fills the centre background possesses all the
immediacy of flesh and blood and the character of incarnate power. In his
nakedness and open-handed stance, we catch too the essential vulnerability
of man, so that in this single picture are gathered up both the fragility and
potency of love, its sacrificial quality and its life-giving dynamic. Eucharist
precisely celebrates such love with its real symbolism of the bread broken
and the wine outpoured.

'His body doubled
under the pack
that sprawls untidily
on his old back,

---

(5)   RABINDRANATH TAGORE *The Hidden God*; quoted by Balasuriya, op. cit.
p. 165

the cold wet deadbeat
plods up the track.
The cook peers out:
"O curse that old lag
here again
with his clumsy swag
made of a dirty
old turnip bag."
"Bring him in cook
from the gray level street
put silk on his body
slippers on his feet,
give him fire
and bread and meat.
Let the fruit be plucked
and the cake be iced,
the bed be snug
and the wine be spiced
in the old cove's nightcap:
for this is Christ."[6]

1.8   Original Sin as Fundamental to the Human Condition

Each section in this chapter has developed the same basic theological stance
as its contribution to a new understanding of central Christian doctrines
and mysteries has been explored. Apart from its place in the total setting
of the book's main thesis, the purpose of outlining such a theology of revelation in its application to a selection of fundamental topics, is to indicate
how a synthesis can be achieved through the rediscovery of an orthodox
view of the mystery of the Incarnation that predates not only the contributions of the Council of Trent but those of Aristotle and Plato as well.

The Christian doctrine of original sin must always play a central part
in a theology that seeks to probe ever more deeply into the mystery of the
relationship between God and man. There is an abiding anxiety that the
proponents of the kind of theology offered in this chapter may be in danger

---

(6)   R. A. K. MASON *On the Swag; in the Wheel: An Anthology of Religious
Verse* ed. Emmiline Garnett (Burns & Oates/Macmillan, 1966) p. 207

of minimising the sheer malice and evil that is rampant throughout the world and a deep-seated possibility in the heart of every man. Is sin regarded as nothing more sinister than an unavoidable difficulty which is part and parcel of a developing cosmos and consciousness — a necessary obstacle in the course of man's journey to his promised end? Among many others, Irenaeus in his day, Duns Scotus in his and most of today's neo-orthodox theologians, especially Teilhard de Chardin, have all challenged this mistaken interpretation of their views, as they increasingly grapple with the strange mystery of sin, its origins and its perenially destructive powers.

This section constitutes a brief introduction to the manner in which some of these theologians have approached a problem that yields no easy or ready-made solutions.

The Purpose of Creation — Adam or Christ?

The question of the origins of sin brings us to a primary question concerning the purpose of creation itself. Did God create so that Adam, the preternatural man, might live for ever without sin, making redemption therefore unnecessary, since without the ambiguously-termed 'happy fault', man would live exactly according to plan? Or did God create Adam knowing that he would fall and so would need a massive rescue operation by Christ in order to re-assemble the radically-shattered original vision of God? There is a third answer to the question — an answer that springs from the theological approach which underpins this chapter. 'Scripture depicts world history as a slow advance towards Christ and his Church and, from the coming of God upon the earth, as a forward march towards the transfiguration of the universe. Christ is at the heart of this account; the universe, whole and entire, has been made in him, through him and for him. Theology too, tries to recover the unity of nature and grace in a christocentric view of the universe and history. In this theology — not new but renewed — Christ and his Church will be seen as the flower of mankind, the masterpiece prepared by God over the course of millions and millions of years. . . .'[1]

Irenaeus in 'Adversus Haereses (III)', reminds us that Paul calls Adam 'the type of the one who was to come' for the Word, maker of all things, has planned beforehand that which would be accomplished in himself — the

---

(1)   RONDET, H. *Original Sin* (Ecclesia Press: 1972) p. 3

economy of the incarnation — for the sons of God. Like Irenaeus, Tertullian saw creation as a form of birth for Christ. In creating Adam, God was tracing a blue-print of himself made man. The Pastoral Constitution on the Church refers us to this statement; 'The shape that the slime of the earth was given was intended with a view to Christ, the future man'[2] Gregory of Nyssa also read the first chapters of Genesis as a prophecy in the past about the present and the future.[3] According to Scotus, God, from all eternity wills to create a universe, and at the centre of this to place man made in his image. This man will be legion and will perpetuate himself by way of generation. But the perfect man, the archetype, will be an exceptional being, so extraordinary that not only will he be almost a god but will be God himself. It is this man who will be the centre of all, his divine person and his humanity being the first objects of God's vision, before the works that are chronologically the most ancient, before the heavens and the earth are created, before the mountains and the hills are established and limits set to the surges of the sea. From all eternity God sees the universe gathered around his son, true man and prototype of all men. He sees him as head of an immense family, as the image of the invisible God, logically preceeding all things.

In terms of Rahner's theological anthropology (cf. section 1.2 above), we briefly considered the notions of obediential potency and the hypostatic union. That consideration should enable us to grasp what he means when he remarks that man is always drafted as the paradigm of the possible utterance of God. He summarises much of his argument in a paragraph which contains four key movements. In short he holds that a) God, in his wish to love and be loved, uttered the Word of love, b) so that it could be heard by virtue of humanity, c) as gift and d) freely responded to. ' . . .God was thinking of the humanity of Christ when he formed Adam. In order to create Adam, God must have had an idea of perfect humanity. For Christians, that perfect humanity was realised in Christ. Christ therefore, was conceived to represent the divine intent which came to historical expression in the creation of Adam.'[4] In *Redemptor Hominis* Pope John Paul II refers to the teaching of the Second Vatican Council; 'The truth is that only in the mystery of the Incarnation does the mystery of man take on light. Christ, the new Adam, in the very revelation of the mystery of the

---

(2)   TERTULLIAN. *De Carnis Resurrectione* (6)
(3)   GREGORY OF NYSSA. *De Hominis Opifico* (1)
(4)   MURPHY O'CONNOR, J. *Becoming Human Together* (Veritas Publications: 1978) p. 48

Father and of his love, fully reveals man to himself and brings to light his most high calling. . . . Man cannot live without love. He remains a being that is incomprehensible for himself, his life is senseless, if love is not revealed to him, if he does not encounter love, if he does not experience it and make it his own, if he does not participate intimately in it. . . .' In his book on the anthropology of St. Paul, Murphy-O'Connor writes 'He (Paul) saw no distinction between Christianity and (true) humanism, because the only way to be authentically human was through Christ. In order to move from the sub-human state of "death" to "life" the person has to be the recipient of the creative love of Christ, and that possibility is grasped only by those who exercise that same creativity for the benefit of others.'[5]

The Purpose of Incarnation — Fulfilment or Redemption?

Rahner maintains that the Fall of man was not the first and only cause of revelation and salvation. He reminds us of the Scotist school of thought which holds that the most basic motive for revelation was not the 'blotting out of sin' but that the Incarnation was already the goal of the divine plan even apart from any divine foreknowledge of freely incurred guilt. The Incarnation may be seen as the most original act of God anticipating the will to create and then to redeem (if necessary), so that redemption from sin would be 'included' in the first desire of God for the hypostatic union, for another way of being Himself, which necessarily called for creation and its conservation. All that is important here, from the point of view of the Church's teaching, is that the victory of the Logos over sin should not be denied. But it is freely permitted to regard the Incarnation, in God's primary intention 'as the summit and height of the divine plan of creation, and not primarily and in the first place as the act of a mere restoration of a divine world-order destroyed by the sins of mankind, an order which God had conceived in itself without any Incarnation.'[6] It also emerges clearly from his ideas about graced nature, constituted in freedom, that the possibility of final damnation by a self-willed self-closure to the meaning of the world and to the meaning of the Word is present to every man. Wherever there is freedom in, and before, the spirit's transcendence towards God there is also the presence of choice whereby this invit-

---

(5)   Ibid. p. 66
(6)   RAHNER, K. *Theological Investigations, Vol. 5.* (Darton Longman & Todd: 1966) p. 185

ing disposal of God towards man can be refused. One could surmise that Rahner would hold that man's fall, as personified in Adam, represents the closedness of man towards God in his self-communicating history; it signifies man's deliberately non-actualised potential leading ultimately to damnation; it expresses independence, rebelliousness and alienation where thankfulness and obedience are called for; it personifies the tendency to refuse the offer of salvation as basically gratuitous and undue, thus seeing man as self-sufficient, capable of initiating his own salvation and finalising his own unaided self-transcendence. The presence of the second Adam before God and man was the direct antithesis of this. He was the only one who was totally open and obedient. He alone offered a full 'yes' to God's call. Christ was the complete answer to the Father's question. Of all men he was, and forever will be, the unique historical member of the human race whose 'fiat' established the final identification of created nature and the uncreated God. Redemption then must not be understood 'as a merely moral or legal transaction, or as a mere non-reckoning of guilt. It is the communication of divine grace and takes place in the ontological reality of God's self-communication. It is therefore, in any case, the continuation and accomplishment of that existential process which consisted from the very beginning in the supernatural pardoning and divinization of humanity.'[7]

The Dogmatic Constitution on Revelation supports this theological stance[8] when it sees Christ as both the completion and salvation of God's first loving desire. 'The God of creation is revealed as the God of Redemption', writes John Paul II in *Redemptor Hominis*, as the 'God who is faithful to himself and faithful to his love for man and for the world, which he revealed on the day of the creation.' In the following passage, Murphy O'Connor gives us an idea of how St. Paul would approach the question. 'All that Adam possessed prior to the Fall was natural to humanity. This natural state was recreated in Christ, and we have seen Paul's insistence that Christ is the norm of humanity. Paul, since he begins, not from humanity as it actually is, but from the divine intention, sees the unfallen state as the natural condition of humanity. The restoration of that state in Christ is a gift, but for him nothing supernatural is involved. Christ in his humanity is precisely what God intended from the beginning, no more and no less.

---

(7)   Ibid. p. 187
(8)   *Documents of Vatican Council II* Dogmatic Constitution on Revelation: arts. 2 & 3. Also cf. Pastoral Constitution on the Church, art. 22

"Life" in the Pauline sense, therefore, is not a grace that raises human nature to a higher level, but simply human nature in its perfection.'[9]

The Source of Sin; original or personal?

In *What are the theologians saying?* M. Hellwig explains that Genesis comments on the human situation in the present not the past; not on how things were in the beginning but on how they are now – the meaning and explanation of man's condition. One sin leads to another, each generation deepens the cloud, all becoming tangled in the universal malaise. 'For John, Jesus is the light that shines into a darkened world where people are no longer able to see things clearly because the powers of darkness have been at work obscuring the reality. In none of the Hebrew or Christian scriptures can you find a clearcut distinction between personal and original sin.'[10] There is no perfectly innocent man because, living in a situation of sin, all become personally entangled to it.

An understanding of sin in general clarifies the notion of original sin. 'Sin is a break with the right order and harmony of God's world which sets things awry in it and complicates life for everybody. To strike another is to arouse anger and evoke a whole chain of violent acts. To be unfaithful in one marriage is to cause a faint, diffuse anxiety in all marriages. To cheat or defraud or betray a secret even once is to start ripples of fear and distrust through the whole society.'[11]

It is not some arbitrary edict of God that people should pay the penalty for the sin of those who went before them. Nor is the transmission of the sin in the act itself of procreation. 'It is because of the way we are constituted that our lives are so largely shaped by those who have lived before us. As individuals we are not made out of nothing but out of history.'[12] No one really starts with a clean slate.

'It is important to distinguish Christian awareness of the mystery of evil, the "sin of the world", from the idea of individual blameworthiness prior to any personal sin. The idea that baptism "forgives original sin" is unknown to the church of the first few centuries. Someone like Tertullian, who was hardly a libertine, felt that the semen of the sexual union transmitted holiness, not sin. And Saint Paul argued that a non-Christian spouse

---

(9)   MURPHY O'CONNOR, J. (op. cit.) p. 60
(10) HELLWIG, M. *What are the Theologians Saying?* (Pflaum: 1970) p. 64
(11) Ibid. p. 65
(12) Ibid. P. 65

is made holy through union with a Christian spouse, on the grounds that the children of a Christian parent are holy, not unclean. Like Tertullian, Paul presupposes that the gift of God's life precedes the mystery of evil, even apart from baptism.'[13]

No-where in the Bible is the term 'original sin' used. The explanation of the term arose with St. Augustine and his defence of infant Baptism. 'The basic scriptural image is that of the "Sin of the world", the general entanglement of mankind in sin, which makes a wall of resistance to the entry of God's light and grace among men. Scripture does not suggest that the sin of the world is passed on to each person by generation, that is by the pro-creative acts that lead to his coming into being. It seems to suggest, rather, that it is passed on by society, culture, upbringing and the experience of human relationships.'[14] It is only now that the damaging confusion of myth and history regarding the Adamic narratives is being dealt with adequately.

Tresmontant has suggested that original sin is not so much the race inheriting the sin of an individual as the individual inheriting the sin of the race. This suggestion is perhaps too facile and is open to mis-interpretation but there is general agreement on the fact that the story of Adam's sin is a message about man, not about the beginning of mankind. It concerns the manner in which man stands before God, not a historical description of how the first man fell before him.

'Adam, theologians agree, is used in the Scriptures as both an individual and as a corporate personality. The sin of Adam, then, is both individual and corporate. In the past, perhaps too much emphasis has been placed on the individual aspect of this sinfulness and not enough on its corporate nature. Humankind as a collectivity is sinful — as one need only read the morning papers to observe. We are born into a race that has piled up a terrible record of sins throughout its past, and that record is part of our cultural and psychic inheritance. In a very real sense the sins of parents are visited upon their children, because the children's personalities are so much the result of parental behaviour and the cultural influences of the society in which children are born. It is a badly flawed heritage that is passed on to us. It is a critically defective human race into which we come. The sinfulness began with the beginning of the human race and has gone on until now. The result is a heritage burdened with evil. However, counter-vailing forces of good have also been at work, alleviating the burden if

(13) GUZIE, T. (op. cit.) p. 168
(14) HELLWIG, M. (op. cit.) p. 66

not eliminating it.'[15] Segundo draws our attention to the two kinds of theology that attempt to explain some of the key 'moments' in salvation-history. There is a difficult trap in the way of those who attempt to link too closely the fact of creation with Eden, the fact of the fall with a couple called Adam and Eve and the beginning of salvation with Jesus Christ. The 'new' theology would look for the meaning of original sin in terms of the fact that man sins and becomes corrupt; the sin of Adam is in our own selves. Man's personal sins ratify and give testimony to the deep-seated malaise within him. This original sinfulness is the deliberate choice for the impersonal, the alienated, the egotistical and the incomplete. It is a 'going astray', a recklessness, a madness, a sickness, as scripture puts it. Something goes wrong in man, an imbalance sets in, a drive grows 'out of true.' Resistance and concupiscence in themselves are neutral, necessary and good. But when out of alignment, man's great spirit can run amok in destruction, confusion and eventually evil. 'These forces of resistance and concupiscence, in their specific meanings and contexts intended here, are not erased by Baptism but rather given the communitarian possibility for opting for synthesis.'[16] While redemption ended the 'enslavement' to sin, it gives us a greater responsibility in our decisions. Baptism, then, is seen as the sacrament of community, and personal growth within it.

---

(15) GREELEY, A. (op. cit.) pp. 63 & 64
(16) SEGUNDO, J.L. *Evolution and Guilt* (Orbis Books: 1974) pp. 51–103

Chapter Two   The Experience of Revelation

2.1   Revelation and Experience as mutually dependent

We are indebted throughout this chapter to G. Baum for his study and presentation of M. Blondel's 'method of immanence' in his search for the 'insider-God.' The presupposition of Blondel's apologetics is the redemptive presence of God to the whole of human life. God is involved where people are. He is present in their growth, in their aspirations, in their movement away from destructiveness to community-awareness and in the extension of their responsibility to include the whole human family. Divine revelation in Jesus Christ is not the addition of new knowledge to human life, introduced from a different world; it rather clarifies and specifies the meaning of man's readiness, from the beginning, for transcendence and transformation. The message of God, uttered in Christ reveals the hidden dynamism present in human life everywhere. The message of salvation is not foreign to man's experience — a message from outside to be accepted on the strength of miracles. The message of salvation ties in with human life: it explains to men what has been and what is going on in their lives and what their destiny is. It enables them to interpret the 'inside talk' that takes place as they listen and respond to the immanent Word, gratuitously present at their deepest centre. Blondel's 'method of immanence', (not to be confused with the 'immanentism' already mentioned), claims that there is no truth which does not arise in some way from man's experience of reality. A message that comes to man wholly from the outside, without an inner and intrinsic relationship to his inmost life, must appear to him as irrelevant, unworthy of attention, unassimilable by the mind and non-believable. No affirmation can be true which does not correspond to the growth and development of the human mind. If there is a transcendent in the finite, then the experience of reality itself and man's sustained reflection on it will eventually lead to its recognition. This 'method of immanence' points towards a methodology for the Incarnational approach. Since man is never totally in possession of himself, never fully all that he could be, he must deal with situation after situation, and experience after experience, in his laying hold on himself on his journey of becoming.

At this point we wish to clarify a little what is meant by the term 'experience' as used by Blondel and Baum in their understanding of Christian revelation. A prophet does not tell people revelations; instead he awakens the revelatory character of their own lives. Revelation is not what certain holy books, holy men or holy institutions possess, it is what communities experience. Neither faith, nor religion, nor revelation can be adequately communicated from outside as a message. But pupils can come to discern the meaning of their own lives with interpretative help from a religious tradition. 'It seems certain that if Buddha, Jeremiah or Jesus were alive today they would not be saying: Exegete these ancient texts and you will know the truth. More likely they would be saying: Look what is happening. Don't trust my pronouncements but listen to what your flesh and blood whisper. It is ecstatically attractive and agonisingly fearful but do not pull away. You are not alone; nature, including human kind, envelopes you. And the one who sent me still lives in the body of man.'[1]

Christians speak of Jesus Christ as the one mediator between God and man, but in the sense that all other forms of mediation are now unnecessary since he has brought mediation to a personal peak. He demonstrated with his life that the divine is mediated in human experience and personal communion. Incarnation would then be the term to describe what is happening in everyone's life. 'The Incarnation of the Word is simply the final term of a creation which is still continuing everywhere'.[2] The experience of creation and evolution is thus seen as the unfolding of incarnation. 'If Christians had kept more in contact with Jewish traditions,' Moran reminds us, 'they would have spoken of incarnation as part of the intention of creation and not as a rescue operation after the introduction of sin.'[3] People who demand that there be a higher norm of truth than human experience are rejecting incarnation and asking for an idol. Man is always tempted to submit to a text or a ruler or an institution. His only other alternative is to follow his own human experience within which he apprehends revelation, and to pursue it wherever it takes him. The Incarnational approach holds that if there be a God who reveals, his voice must be heard within the experience of a man who listens with all other men for the voice of the divine. There is something more to his experience than *what* he experiences. 'Experience is less what a man has than what a man addresses and what mankind is addressed by.'[4]

There is an element in experience that can never be put into direct focus, yet in many attempts at experience-based teaching in R.E., it is

(1)   MORAN G. *The Present Revelation*: (Herder & Herder, 1972) pp. 228f
(2)   de CHARDIN T. *Christianity and Evolution* (Collins, 1971) p. 53
(3)   MORAN *op. cit.* p. 270
(4)   MORAN *Design for Religion* (Search Press, 1971) p. 45

regarded as something which the pupils have had and so, a useful jumping-off point for wherever the teacher wishes to go. This is a disturbing feature of many experience-based curricula in R.E. The very depth that is sought for is often, by definition, eliminated. 'The error of empiricism,' G. Marcel wrote, 'is to take experience for granted and to ignore the mystery; whereas what is amazing and miraculous is that there should be experience at all.'[5] All kinds of implications may be overlooked by the life-theme which rushes in pursuit of the facts of experience. There are many, too, who un-consciously fear this whole exercise.'This hidden dimension of self, sought for centuries by men who have longed for personal fulfillment beyond rationalism, is usually dreaded by the average person. It could be called 'experiencing possibility.' It sometimes 'peeps out' when one permits one-self to be unfocussed and aimless, unintegrated, not going anywhere or doing anything; but it is 'tamped back' in anxious haste for it is experienced like the contents of Pandora's box.'[6] Moran strikes a topical and central note when he concludes that 'the understanding or misunderstanding of the category of experience gives rise to two different educational anthro-pologies. The first will try to locate thinking elements within experience that would modify behaviour in a way not entirely predictable. The second will seek to get a person to think in a way that will make his behaviour conform to some standard.'[7]

2.2   An example from Doctrine

The following paragraphs are offered as a brief outline of how revelation directly contributes to the heightening of man's self-awareness. They are offered, too, as another example of the kind of objectives that are central to the Incarnational approach to the life-theme. Following on Baum, we select the notion of the Trinity — God as Father, God as Word and as Spirit — because it is a notoriously difficult *doctrine* to apprehend as ex-plaining and intensifying human experience, and yet it is at the heart of all specifically sacramental and generally liturgical Christian celebration. Beyond the addition of another truth about God to be believed by the human intellect, where is the personal transformation of consciousness in

(5)   MARCEL G. *The Philosophy of Existentialism* (The Citadel Press, 1962) p. 128
(6)   JOURARD S. *Disclosing Man to Himself* (Van Nostrand, 1968) p. 45
(7)   MORAN *Design for Religion: op. cit.* p. 65

the new awareness of this triple relationship entered into and re-affirmed by the Christian in the sacraments of Baptism and Eucharist? How does one follow the suggestion of 'the new theologians' and translate these dogmatic statements into liberating insights about human experience and consiousness?

Whether one is engaged in teaching religion with a view to deepening the commitment of the pupils or to enlightening others about Christianity, the Incarnational approach would present the faith in terms of a new consciousness created within the believer. The acceptance of God as Father, for instance, induces, in the Christian, a transformation of consciousness and a modification of self-experience and orientation towards the world. The author of reality is not hostile or indifferent. The ground of being is not a waste-land. Despite evil and injustice, the ultimate principle of total reality is love itself. There is meaning and purpose in life. Destruction can be controlled. Protection is available. The Christian is aware of himself as a son. Therefore he has a destiny. A Christian teenager may then say: 'In spite of my isolation and self-rejection; in spite of the blindness and ignorance of others; in spite of the temptation to exploit a hostile world for my own ends, belief in God as Father offers me, as son, the possibility of growing and sharing, of believing in myself and my destiny, of accepting, rejoicing in and loving myself.' G. Baum points out the political aspect of the acceptance of this revealed doctrine. 'To believe that God is Father means to believe that men are destined to be brothers and that salvation is at work in their history. God revealing himself as Father discloses to us the salvational meaning of history and thus changes our basic orientation to the world around us.'[8]

In God's self-revelation, he emerges as Word. To believe that God is Word means to believe that man is a listener. One cannot come to self-knowledge alone. Each person must be told who he is by another. Hence the point of revelation. Because God's Word was fully enunciated in Christ the creature, the Christian recognises that all creatures and experiences are revelatory. In all situations he identifies a voice speaking to him. He hears words in all his senses. Here is the true basis of the life-theme. Here, too, is the neglected aspect of the excellent structures for moral education where revelation is divorced from experience. 'A man who experiences himself as a listener will enter every conversation, every human relationship, every manifestation of human art and wisdom, with the readiness to discern the

---

(8)   BAUM G. *Faith and Doctrine* (Newman Press, 1969) p. 20

voice that calls him to greater self-knowledge and strengthens him to grow in his humanity.'[9] The world is no longer silent. A man's decisions are full of information about him. The Christian will recognise the message present in all his experiences; the message to remain open to the meaning hidden in life itself. He will listen then to the story of the pain in his life and realise that wisdom and meaning are costly graces. He hears in Christ the meaning God offers to every human life; he hears too that death and resurrection are the passage way to self-transcendence – death to the old destructive drive that a man clings to, resurrection to new dimensions that a man fears. The possibilities here for authentic life-themes are endless, where the central core of the curriculum *has* to be experience-based, and where these experiences are not just explored, but explained, focused, intensified and multiplied by Christian revelation.

Finally, how does the revealed truth that God is Spirit – a truth that is repeated in one form or another of Trinitarian symbolism at every as-sembly, sacramental celebration and liturgical prayer and worship-service – when rationally analysed, purify and enrich human experience. Many current life-themes, on 'Loneliness', for instance, in the presentation of the Christian religion, have very responsibly drawn on absorbing situations as portrayed in novels, films, songs and personal experience, in the effort to analyse this life-sapping experience. Among the objectives would be the provision for the pupil of the skill of coping with his own sense of rejection and fear, by introducing him to the universality of these conditions and to some of the concepts and demands of brotherhood and community-awareness. Christian educators, such as J. Holm and M. Grimmitt for example, would probably regard this exercise, in itself, as R.E.[10] No explicit reference is made, except in passing, to any specific religious contribution towards a more thorough understanding of the experience. Others again, perhaps those following a more conventional approach will highlight the message of the Gospel concerning the Christian's obligation in love and duty to combat loneliness, build community and praise the Lord. The Incarnational approach, however, would search out the nature of the new consciousness that revelation bestows on this particular human condition. It would see God as Spirit (the Third Person), present deep within each one, creating life out of death. The Christian belief in the Trinity affirms

---

(9)   *Ibid:* p. 22
(10) HOLM J. *Teaching Religion in School* (Oxford University Press 1975) cf. Ch. 5
      GRIMMITT, M. What Can I do in R.E.? (Mayhew-McCrimmon, 1973) cf.
      Ch. 5

that the spirit of Jesus, the love of the Father, is always at work in men producing the new creation. Man is not trapped in the world, ensnared in his loneliness, the victim of his temperament and fear. His fear is that the limitations and compulsions of his inner life and basic drives will determine his future; that the stifling patterns of today's isolation will predetermine the shape of tomorrow's existence. The revelation that God is Spirit guarantees a source of power and healing within each tormented soul. This conviction, this new consciousness of the existential reality of the risen Spirit, when internalised and deeply accepted, brings a radical change and transformation in the Christian's presence to himself and others. It is, as Rahner wrote, at the finest points of strength or fracture that the event of grace is taking place, that the new really happens. Man is more than man. There is a principle, operative in his experience, that transcends him. Christ's divinity, too, emerged not in the fact of the absence of loneliness, fear and anxiety in his life, but in the way he coped with them and, by understanding them, realised the inevitability of their presence and the gifts which they hid. It is in the culmination of Incarnation — the crisis moment of Calvary when the spirit-filled humanity of Jesus resisted the last challenge of non-being in the form of despair, hopelessness and loneliness — that the Christian finds the strange revelation, that for every man salvation comes only in the meeting of a challenge and in the risk of experience of failure. Can one hold that part of the strange mystery lies in the fact that there is much about God which, when fleshed into time and space, can emerge only as loneliness and suffering?

2.3   An example from Liturgy

The Christian Eucharist, for example, is a primary factor in perpetuating into the present and the future, the once-for-all historical revelation in Christ, that God offers transformation to men in the ordinary situations of life. It means that every meal is intended to be a means of grace. If a man has not learned what it is to eat in fellowship with others he will never truly celebrate Eucharist. The Eucharist judges the quality of one's presence at any meal. It stands as a perpetual demand for the dialogue and communion that should characterise all human inter-action so often characterised in one's attitude to the shared meal. The Eucharist sensitises us to the hidden and saving presence of God in all aspects of life. It tells us not simply how Christ is present to the Church as it gathers for worship; it tells us what God offers to men who eat at the same table, engage in human conversation and enjoy the same gifts in common. Eating together can be a redemptive happening.

Our reasons for holding to these convictions have been considered in much greater depth in Chapter One. The general development is as follows. The Christian believes that every act of Christ was open to the self-communication of God. The human nature which he holds in common with all men is defined in terms of this openness and self-transcendence — its capacity for self-surrender in pursuit of the possible achievement of its own true identity. Christ's unique identity was fully realised in the course of his life. In what is called the hypostatic union of God and man, of the logos and human nature, of the sacred and the secular, the potential of Jesus Christ, and so of all men, was irrevocably realised — '. . .that man might become God.' This destiny of all men depends on their openness to the constantly offered being of God, always mediated through human experience, as it was for Christ. In a ritual involving bread, wine and words, Christians remember, affirm and celebrate that fact of belief. This ceremony encapsulates in time and space, in one privileged and symbolic moment, the eternal significance of time-bound existence. It is precisely because there is an element of this revelatory function in every meal that all great religions and cultures incorporate eating and drinking into the ceremonial celebration of their most cherished convictions.

Whereas many current R.E. approaches set out to explain and explore the hidden significance of a meal with a view to either laying a foundation for a deeper understanding later on of a more specifically religious experience (e.g. the Eucharist) or else to discover the modified form of revelation within the secular experience itself, independently of the Christ-event, the Incarnational Approach centres on the reality and totality of the experience itself. For instance, does a man nourish or poison himself and others every time he sits at a common table? What does one's manner of sharing a meal indicate about his attitudes to life? Is a person growing in openness or feeding his self-sufficiency in the process of eating with others?

Like any human activity eating is ambiguous. It can be a self-destructive exercise. A man may devour his food to feed his isolation. Compulsive eating may be a willed distraction from facing responsibility. The unconscious wish to remain a baby, and so dependent, may be the source of many an appetite. 'Eating together could be an enforced coming together of people who try to avoid one another all day, accompanied by a carefully screened conversation by which each tries to keep the other out of his life, a nervous juggling with words, interrupted occasionally by jokes that hurt and remarks by which one triumphs over another, until the longed-for moment arrives when everyone rises from the table, each to his own island life.'[11] Such meals are caricatures of the ideal. They are negative and diminishing influences from which man needs salvation. They feed sickness and nourish scepticism; they encourage the fear of trust and risk. They accuse us of complicity in the awful fact that vast numbers of men are hungry. Eating, on the other hand, is redemptive when it is an acknowledgement of the need of food and so, of other people. Even the farmer needs a communal table. People need people. Eating means opening oneself to others and to otherness. The desire for food is no respecter of persons. It is the great leveller. Not many can be proud and hungry at the same time. Eating may be seen as sacramental when a meal shared with others offers men redemption from their pride and individualism and opens them to the human community. God is the good news that community is possible. This too is what Eucharist means. The original sin of man lies in his lack of hunger for communion.'The only real fall of man is his non-eucharistic life in a non-eucharistic world.'[12] When people eat together the eucharistic mystery is offered to them — the invitation to affirm the healing and inner rebuilding constantly at work amongst the wounds inflicted by their self-centredness, a salvation that is guaranteed in the Incarnation.

What needs to be shown here, and shown to be orthodox, is the fact that something like a Copernican revolution has taken place in our understanding of revelation and sacrament. Instead of an intellectual and sprititual movement from the sacramental event towards its effect in the world, a spiritual movement of the world towards the sacrament can now be discerned, or rather is once more being rediscovered as central to the authentic and original Christian revelation.

Taking the notion of 'sacrament' in its widest sense, the common meal is often a sacramental moment for man. It encapsulates much more than the empirical happenings and interchange of the actual occasion. It can be a significant moment of emergence and revelation concerning the growth or withering of how a person relates to the world, to others and to himself. It can betray a great deal about the openness or closedness of

---

(11)   BAUM, G. *Man Becoming* (Herder & Herder, 1971) p. 71
(12)   SCHMEMANN, A. *The World as Sacrament* (Darton, Longman & Todd 1974) p. 19

one's fundamental option, indicating an attitude of gratitude and life, or fear and death. This holds equally true for the child's lunch-time apple and the executive's extravagant banquet. The shared meal is a key revelatory moment of whether humanity and community are being set free and allowed to be, or whether egoism and isolation are dominant. This is how it pertained, too, for the communal meals in the course of Christ's human life. It is because the Christian believes that the break-through of Christ's humanness into glory was achieved through his obedience to his own graced and growing nature — a break-through that consisted, among other things, in the knowledge he gained of his own identity through communion with others in the experience of shared meals with all kinds of displaced people as well as with his friends — that he also believes, since he, too, shares in the same basic humanity of Christ — a humanity destined for the same glory — that all his experiences, particularly that of eating together with his fellow-man are 'peak-joint' sources and opportunities of discovering whether he too is on the ultimate road to salvation or 'damnation'. In this context, the Eucharist is the gentle reminder, in the face of man's strange desire towards self-centredness and aloneness, that only in the service and true love of himself and others is progress in graced humanity and community, and so, paradoxically, in genuine self-fulfilment, as God's image, possible.

The Incarnational Approach suggests that the R.E. teacher, whether following an 'implicit' or 'explicit' method (as long as it is not in any way indoctrinatory) presents a picture of the Christian at the Eucharist as one who is profoundly aware of the drama into which his life is unceasingly drawn, the drama of the world, the divine Tragedy and the divine Comedy. 'He thinks of the dying, those facing their end glassy-eyed and with the death-rattle in their throat, and he knows that this fate has already taken up lodging in his own being. He feels in himself the groaning of the creature and the world, their demand for a more hopeful future. He grasps something of the burden borne by statesmen, their responsibility for decisions demanding all their courage and yet whose effects will be extending into an unknown future. He bears within himself something of the laughter of children in their unshadowed future-laden joy: within him resounds also the weeping of the starving children, the agony of the sick, the bitterness caused by betrayed love. The dispassionate seriousness of the scientist in his laboratory, the hard determination of those struggling to liberate mankind — all these find their echo in him. And even when this is all unavailable to him, when the shallowness of his existence and the sterility of his heart are *incapable* of opening themselves here and now to this whole weight of human history — even here he remains painfully aware that this narrow-minded, shallow and sterile life of his is still demanding once again to be filled with all these things that move the world and affect men's lives. And he is not astonished when the mysterious reality of world history, with its strange, stupefying and yet exciting power, rises from the depths of his existence and floods the country of his heart.'[13]

The Christian offers up the world under the form of bread and wine, Rahner points out, knowing that the world is already constantly offering itself up to the incomprehensible God under its own forms, in the ecstasy of its joy and the bitterness of its sorrow. He receives under holy signs the Body of the Lord knowing this to be worthless were he not to communicate with that other Body of God which is the world itself and its fate.

2.4   An example from man's nature

The third example concerns a more common and secular depth-experience. *Friendship*, too, is an experience that is memorable, the source of many decisions and the principle of unity in life. A life-theme following the Incarnational Approach would investigate all these characteristics, exploring the demands and dangers of close encounters of this kind. The depth of one's vulnerability is exposed in friendship — the fear of trusting, the reluctance to surrender. This demands the courage to be open and the risk of being rejected. Self-knowledge in these circumstances brings self-possession and harmony within. A transformation takes place and two people discover new depths to their beings that were unsuspected previously. By this I mean that a relationship, if it is genuine, calls forth what is latent in each partner. By drawing out what was there, but not formerly realised, each person is strengthened because the reality of his own person is now more accessible, and this in turn speaks to deeper reaches in the non-actualised capacities of the other. 'Disclosure begets disclosure,' S. Jourard writes, 'I believe that trust and hope are not *contributors* to healing. Rather they are the experienced aspect of a *total* organismic healing or re-integration process. Trust and hope are indications that the healing or re-integration or self-transcendence process *has been set in motion*. Trust and hope don't

---

(13)   RAHNER, K. *Secular Life and the Sacraments* (The Tablet, Vol. 225, No. 6823, March 1971) p. 267

cause healing. They *are* healing.'[14] The Incarnation explains this. It was in the uniting of parts, the harmony of 'persons' that the hypostatic wholeness became the paradigm for all dividedness. The divided self cannot mend itself alone. Man is born broken. He bears the birth-mark of self-centredness. N. Brown, in *Love's Body*, repeatedly quotes W. B. Yeats: 'Nothing can be sole or whole, that has not been rent.'[15] The healing of the rent in the whole is at the heart of reality. But man cannot escape his dividedness alone. By his own will-power alone a man is incapable of making himself selfless. Each man's 'thou' is the bringer of salvation, as M. Buber has clarified.[16] It is not so much *what* is given from one to the other, because 'no *what* is really given at all,' as Jourard points out. Grace is activated. The mystery of salvation is happening when people lose a grain of their egoism in the mutual redemption of friendship. Whether they know it or not, the Christian holds, people who through growth and reconciliation become friends, participate in the paschal mystery of the Incarnation; the death and resurrection of Christ become operative in their lives. 'We may note,' writes Moran, 'that the religious traditions usually speak of healing, saving or redeeming as central to the religious process. Often, however, there is little intrinsic connection between the healing element and revelation. In fact, in Christian theology, they have usually emerged as quite separate processes. One of the indications that revelation was inadequately understood is shown by the fact that revelation was not of itself a healing process.'[17] The Incarnational approach endeavours to redress this balance.

Developing friendships, as well as established ones, (even amongst the very young), stand in need of purification and vigilance. 'Self-seeking, ambition, destructive sensuality or the desire for power may colour the experience of friendship so that, instead of promoting growth and rec-onciliation, it actually nourishes the destructive and hostile trends in men.'[18] The Incarnational approach to an experience-based curriculum would investigate all these ever-present forces and tendencies. Revelation in Christ, as well as establishing the infinite possibilities within human

---

(14) JOURARD, S. *Disclosing Man to Himself* (Van Nostrand, 1968) pp. 23 & 68 Quoted by MORAN op. cit. p. 90

(15) BROWN N. *Love's Body* (Random Press 1966) p. 80

(16) BUBER M. *I and Thou* (Clark, 1971) p. 11

(17) MORAN *The Present Revelation* p. 90

(18) BAUM *Faith and Doctrine* p. 75

nature for self-transcendence, signals too, the insidious capacity of man for self-deception and self-delusion.

It is with these final thoughts on some further human aspects of revelation and friendship that we bring this section to a close. 'Between two human beings, to the degree that there is revealing, there is healing,' writes Moran. He continues to point out that if the process does not move in the direction of healing, then what is going on is not a revealing of persons. It is more likely a concentration on revealing certain things which are actually a mask to prevent a revealing of the person. What was revealed in Christ, and what is the horizon that all human self-revelations are judged and measured against, is the total integrity of words, actions and self-hood that culminated in his once-for-all and unsurpassable break-through into all men's possible destiny. As with Christ, true revelation is a slow process. 'Every attempt to unveil the truth is at once a veiling and unveiling of the whole truth. Revelation, as human beings experience it, is always in part a process of concealing. One might expect that revelation makes everything clear and eliminates mystery. Religious spokesmen often seem to suppose just that, but if they looked closely at human relationships they would see otherwise.'[19] A life-theme on 'friendship' would explore this aspect of revelation within a relationship and the part that relationship plays in revelation. Pupils would be helped to see that human beings cannot reveal themselves totally nor can they place themselves into clear words and unambiguous gestures. The attempt at instant disclosure, to strip the psyche bare all at once, is tied to the fear of what is left unexposed in oneself or others. Hence the games people play. 'Talking a great deal,' said Nietzsche, 'is a way of concealing oneself.'[20] One of the basic contributions of the Incarnational approach to a 'secular' life-theme exercise such as we are considering here, is that it would regard this exploration into the delicate undergrowth of friendship as the necessary preamble to a clearing and pruning of roots and branches, in the interests of procuring a healthy growth. At no stage does it move on into the cultivated pastures of 'spiritual' love and disembodied friendship. Its only interest is in adding colour and dimension to what is actually happening in the lives of the pupils, and it never strays from the arena of human experience. It was, for instance, in the ordinary experience of human friendship with Jesus Christ that his apostles began to

---

(19)   MORAN *op. cit.* p. 91
(20)   NIETZSCHE *Beyond Good and Evil* quoted by G. Moran, op. cit.: p. 91

understand the deeper significance of this relationship.[21] They experienced revelation precisely within this relationship and indeed it was in the very same interaction that the new consciousness of who he himself was became apparent to Jesus.

To avoid the possibility of 'Christian revelation' being regarded as 'something,' Moran prefers to speak of 'a universal revelation which finds expression in lived relationships.'[22] He would see Incarnation as the revelation of the redemption accomplished within all authentic human relationships. The sacred is the eternal guarantee of the autonomy of the secular, and achieves itself only to the degree that the secular achieves itself. The emergence of an autonomous and creative secularity is the result of the 'yes' of God in Jesus Christ, to his own creation. God alone can create things which can stand by themselves before his face. To the extent that radical dependence on him increases, so does independence of him increase. 'It is only because God can assume something and still preserve its non-divinity, its humanity and its worldliness that he was pleased to create the world and then to assume it in the Word. The Incarnation, then, is a liberation of the humanness of Jesus and in him the liberation of the world and man to find their own proper existence in order to become fully themselves.'[23] It is because Christ emptied himself of his humanity, not his divinity, that the Christian has a unique contribution to make to a theme on friendship. Man finds himself by giving himself away. Human friendship and relationship is an exercise in this dying to self. The more that someone loses himself and is thus accepted as friend by another, the more does he become himself and the more powerfully are his possibilities stirred to realisation. The interpenetration of person and person in human love is such that there is unity in the very duality, without mutual absorption or reduction. The only dualism that is acceptable for the Christian in a consideration of friendship as a theme in R. E., is not that between human and divine love but between truly human and sub-human love. A theme on friendship in the context of education into the Christian understanding of this relationship will reveal that the painful process of loving someone else is already, and in itself, the coming into being of true humanism and therefore of God. The necessary and rational explanation, purification and intensification of this understanding lies totally, and only, for the Christian, in the hard fact that it has already happened in Jesus Christ.

---

(21)   cf. MORAN *Theology of Revelation* (Burns & Oates, 1967) pp. 77

(22)   MORAN *The Present Revelation* p. 118

(23)   CHERESO, J. *The Sacred Secular* (Pflaum, 1969) p. 73

PART TWO

An Educational Theory for the Incarnational Approach

Chapter Three An Analysis of Meaning

3.1 The Contribution of Philip Phenix

'It is not easy to sustain a sense of the Whole.'[1] With this opening statement Philip Phenix not only pinpoints the problem of constructing a
general and properly integrated curriculum; he touches on the radical
human predicament relating to all our experience of life. It is natural for
the human mind to seek an overall synthesis; to create a totality from the
numerous partial syntheses arrived at through knowledge and experience.
Nevertheless, it is a quest that, for most, is satisfied only in occassional
glimpses of the interrelatedness of all meanings: perhaps by listening to a
powerful symphony, or reading a moving poem, hearing a great speaker, or
viewing a beautiful landscape. These moments of 'going beyond' as Maslow
describes it, constitute peak experiences in our existence. We feel somehow
that here in this experience, all that we understand by reality coheres. On
the other hand, we are unable to maintain our hold on this greater synthesis;
its very vastness prevents us. We find ourselves reduced once more to 'knowing in part', our vision is 'through a glass darkly'. As Martin Heinecken
observes: 'The individual in his existence as time and eternity is constantly
still on the way, in the process of becoming what in another sense he
already is, constantly riding the crest of the wave of decision.'[2] (Cf.
Ch. 1.2) It is thus that most of us, most of the time, endeavour to live and
to grow by degrees towards a level of self-integration.

The general aim of education therefore is the integrated personality
and all that is offered to the child should serve this end. It is not enough,
observes Phenix, merely that we *recognise* the real relationship and cross-
reference of all curricular components; they should also be properly
established by well thought out teaching methods directed at integration.
Not only is man a seeker of organised meaning for whom the curriculum

---

(1)   PHILIP PHENIX *Realms of Meaning* (McGraw-Hill, 1964) p. 1
(2)   MARTIN HEINECKEN *The Moment Before God;* p. 361

ought to reflect a corresponding organic quality, governed by the objective of human wholeness; he is, moreover, a community creature and the principles for community growth will tend to disintegration if the curriculum 'compartmentalises' its components. Man is a many-sided animal. There are, suggests Phenix, a variety of angles from which he is capable of viewing the world — as natural scientist, social scientist, artist, moralist, historian, theologian or philosopher. Man communicates through language and culture; he is a creature of feeling, celebration and anticipation. Across all these capacities and characteristics runs the distinctive and unifying feature of man — his ability to *think*. This is to be defined, Phenix claims, not in the narrow sense of logical mental processes and intellectual development, but within the broader understanding of man as a seeker of *meaning*. All his activities of mind and heart: reason, feeling, awareness, conscience, inspiration are directed towards the discovery of meaning. In the education field we should promote the growth of integrated patterns of meaning by which the child might learn personal and social integration.

This is not an easy task. No-one with a degree of sensitivity can fail to discern, in the pressures of contemporary culture, the conflicting pole of meaninglessness in our paradoxical quest for meaning. Paul Tillich's analysis of human anxiety associated with finitude, relativism, futility and disillusionment[3]; Viktor Frankl's concern for rediscovering hope and faith in life by means of his 'logotherapy' method[4] — these writers highlight for all involved in education the problems to be faced in our modern world. A successful curriculum must seek imaginatively to overcome the prevalent forces of meaninglessness and to aid in unifying our fragmented experience.

Nevertheless, some educationists would claim certain difficulties in Phenix's concept of meaning and these must be examined if we are to prove the usefulness of his analysis to the Incarnational approach. Are we to assign a *cognitive* character to 'meaning'? What proportion of our claims to 'knowledge', particularly in the religious sphere, in fact amount to belief or intuition by which our lives are rendered meaningful? Paul Hirst, with his theory of the 'forms of knowledge,' seeks to maintain an objectivity of analysis founded on the assumption that the criteria for the conceptual structure of language is that which can be *known*, rather that simply believed, felt or fancied.[5] Each 'form' — whether the empirical, mathematical,

(3)   PAUL TILLICH *The Courage To Be* (Fontana, 1964)
(4)   VIKTOR FRANKL *The Doctor and the Soul* (Pelican, 1973)
(5)   ALLEN BRENT *Philosophical Foundations for the Curriculum* (Unwin, 1978)

philosophical, moral, aesthetic, religious or historical — constitutes a unique category of knowledge, identified as such by a network of concepts logically autonomous from those of other forms. Hirst contends that Phenix confuses a general type of knowing on the one hand with vague states of awareness and perception on the other.[6] It seems that in seeking to classify in one fell swoop the propositional sphere and the realm of existential awareness, Phenix introduces into the dimension of knowledge elements that properly belong to another dimension.

We would suggest however that Hirst's analysis, though quite consistent in itself, is perhaps founded on too rigid an interpretation of the human apprehension of reality. (Cf. Ch. 1.2) If humanity has as its heart the mystery which makes men capable of knowing, loving and creating, then a more flexible analysis which withholds clear distinctions between the cognitive and the affective, knowledge and meaning, would seem to be more appropriate. (Cf. Ch. 3.3) We propose that the contribution of Phenix is extremely valuable in that he recognises the threat to the unique and mysterious character of man implicitly presented by such categorisation. Moran warns us that 'the attempt to imitate methods of positive science and mathematics has led to the apotheosis of "pure objectivity" as the ideal of knowledge and the consequent abstraction of intellectual activity from the rest of man's life.'[7] This abstraction is founded on a false interpretation of the human person. Indeed, when we speak of the education of the emotions and feelings for instance, it would be absurd to imagine that we can drive a logical wedge between what the child feels and what he knows or should know. That would be a sure way to induce schizoid disorder — clearly contrary to our aim of wholeness and integration. Cannot a case in fact be made for some kind of intrinsic association between propositional thought and feeling or awareness in the unifying subject? This will be the area of discussion in the third section of the present chapter.

---

(6)   PAUL HIRST *Knowledge and the Curriculum* (Routledge & Keegan Paul, 1966)
(7)   GABRIEL MORAN *What is Revelation?* (Theological Studies 1965) p. 220

3.2   Language and Meaning

Living experience possesses an immediacy which structured knowledge does not have. This can frequently be seen in the reactions of a young child exploring new objects, tasting or touching certain foods or substances, or simply regarding the face of a stranger. In the context of explicitly religious experience it is no less true that children can have sharply intuitive moments which are nonetheless real for being unstructured and perhaps only vaguely communicable. The following passage, recollecting a childhood experience of this nature, indicates the possibility of an overarching vision which we feel is particularly acute in the young: 'The strong feeling which characterised my experiences invariably was a feeling of meaning. I felt myself, for a fleeting moment, to be part of the world of meaning, unrestricted by space and time and the limitations of my physical space-suit, part of a world where all was known and all was understood, all was acknowledged, appreciated, loved, with a love vastly transcending worldly concepts. Obviously I could not have put this into words.'[8] Though this sense of meaning can only properly be shared in later and retrospective attempts at conceptualisation, this by no means renders the original awareness meaningless *for the child*. By overstressing the cognitive and the explicitly conceptual in the religious dimension, we run the risk of using language to make reality more articulate than it is. This highlights the dangers of compelling the child to interpret his experience for us by way of verbal description. The metaphorical extensions of meaning constituted by language can never be completely satisfactory in terms of the total reality of the child's awareness. 'We may learn to live with mystery more significantly,' maintains Marcel, 'to penetrate more and more profoundly its nature, but however deeply we enter into it and discern its secrets, the mystery remains mysterious.'[9] We should take cognizance of other media of communication which may be more appropriate forms of expression for religious feeling in the child and ultimately result in a more integrated understanding of what we are teaching him. Art, music and movement for instance are most important in the R.E. curriculum.

Normally however our sense of reality can only fully develop through the use of living language. Man in community requires the symbols of language to incarnate thought. As the chief means of self-expression and

(8)   EDWARD ROBINSON *The Original Vision* (RERU, 1977) p. 55
(9)   GABRIEL MARCEL *Philosophy of Existence* (Arno, 1949), quoted in V. Madge, Children in Search of Meaning, (S.C.M. 1965)

self-actualisation, as well as for the furtherance of relationships, language is a central ingredient for creating and consolidating community. The dilemma for religious education has always been whether or not there is a precise form of religious language by which 'religious knowledge' is communicated. Can we in fact legitimize our R.E. only in terms of a vocabulary which relates to other-worldly realities; that is, by specific theological concepts such as grace, soul, the infinite and so on? 'God is the supreme Being who alone exists of Himself and is infinite in all perfections.' So goes the Catechism statement. But just how intelligible can this be to the child? Having largely acknowledged the constraints of a purely doctrinal procedure, we have seen the emergence of the life-theme approach as an extremely valuable corrective. Most of the current schemes and syllabuses would seem to be based in one way or another on this method.

The life-theme approach, however, itself appears frequently to be hamstrung by the problem of language — or more accurately the problem of two languages. In turn this issue finds its roots in the fundamental dualism which characterises a scholastic and essentialist kind of theology as discussed in chapter one(1.1). The real anxiety surrounding life-theme teaching is that it has not quite recognised its own theological rationale. (Cf. Ch. 5.5, 5.6) 'Life-talk' still seems to be one kind of language expressing realities immediately identified within the experience of the child — friends, pets, work, hobbies, loneliness, etc. 'God-talk' on the other hand is another set of categories, not easily identifiable in experiential terms. Our 'life-talk' is often referred to as a sort of preparation or preamble to explicit religious concepts, which almost unconsciously we regard as the *real* religious content of our teaching. An Incarnational theology seeks to overcome this dichotomy of language on the basis of its unified and existential understanding of revelation. 'Religious truth,' observes M.V.C. Jeffreys, 'is normal experience understood at fullest depth; what makes truth religious is not that it relates to some abnormal field of thought or feeling but that it goes to the roots of the experience which it seeks to interpret.'[10] Christian theology and in the same way the R.E. teacher must probe 'the nature of the human existent, his hopes and loves, his finitude and sin, in the conviction that the study of man in depth opens up the dimension of transcendence.'[11]

Language therefore is truly religious to the extent that it expresses

---

(10)   JEFFREYS, M.V.C. *Glaucon* (Pitman, 1961) p. 118
(11)   JOHN MACQUARRIE *Existentialism* (Penguin, 1972) p. 271

and communicates the deepest reality and meaning of human experience. 'Language is made for expressing the thoughts of the heart and for uniting people. But when it is the prisoner of prefabricated formulas, in its turn it drags the heart along downward paths. One must act upon language therefore in order to act upon the heart and to avoid the pitfalls of language.'[12] A resonant use of language symbols is more significant than the concepts employed. This is because the verbal, whether couched in 'religious' or 'secular' terms is always a pointer to the nonverbal, an interpretation of the actual experience of the subject. Hubert Halbfas applies this analysis of the 'how' rather than the 'what' of language in his much underrated book of the late sixties, *Theory of Catechetics*, subtitled *Language and Religious Experience*. He deserves quoting at length. 'A language which does not speak in terms of the world cannot speak the truth. If faith is rooted in the single reality, in our history and age, and if God does not exist outside this reality but only within it, all genuine discussion of God must be discussion of the world. There is no such thing as a sacred language which opens the depths of reality and yet exists on a different plane from secular language. Talk of God is not talk *about* God but of our own involvement in God. . . . Language is never "religious" through its subject matter but only through its quality. . . . Only men who talk about themselves, about what faces them and concerns them in the "here and now", can talk about God. The truth of God is concrete. . . . To talk about God you do not have to use theological terms. The word "God" itself is often unnecessary. . . . Talking about one's wife, learning to live with an illness, saying what work really means to one, sharing one's love for a painting or a poem: all this can be talk of God. It is not the "what" that gives human language this "content", but its "how". Some people just speak about children, their house and garden, supper and bed, and yet their discourse is full of faith and hope, thanks and prayer. . . . The "content" of religious discourse is God, but it is not this *word*, together with the vocabulary of Church doctrine that communicates God, but only the life-revealing language of one's fellow men.'[13] All this is so, Halbfas insists, because 'proclaiming the truth of Jesus of Nazareth, of the Christ . . . also means that everything is not restricted to Jesus of Nazareth, but that Jesus of Nazareth is the justification — the legitimation — for speaking about God in concrete terms, that is, "in the flesh".' Meaning

---

(12)   JOHN PAUL II *World Peace Day Speech*, Jan. 1979; quoted in *The Pope from Poland: An Assessment*, ed. J. Whale (Fontana, 1980) p. 46
(13)   HUBERT HALBFAS *Theory of Catechetics* (Herder & Herder, 1971) pp. 57. 136–7

then can be communicated through whatever language forms are qualitatively transparent of it. As Doug Crutchfield says in the film *Dancing Prophet*: 'You can say God a thousand times a day and never mean a thing.'[14] The decisive factor is the love that determines all our communications, verbal and nonverbal, and the extent to which dogmatic formulations, when used, are directed at illuminating life as it is lived. Unless we fully recognise the integrity of all reality by rejecting the 'two planes' model, we will always tend to abstract and remove the language of doctrine from actual human existence and under these conditions we cannot expect the emergence of truly religious meaning. 'The criterion of religious communication is the freedom that it gives, that is, the humanity that it offers. Wherever discourse occurs in the name of God without men becoming happier, more hopeful, and more profoundly capable of love, even though the "word of God" is defined dogmatically, it does not come to pass.'[15]

These considerations of language and meaning lead us to investigate briefly the nature of that extremely important linguistic medium of communication, the story. Our imaginative faculties enable us to create possible worlds and characters beyond that which we know as the concrete and actual; to combine various aspects of our knowledge and interpretation of existence into a new creation which nevertheless echoes our own deepest being and reflects our strongest aspirations and ideals. The myths and fantasies which have permeated the history of mankind since time immemorial testify to this. Expression of religious truths has always been an inextricable mixture of history and myth, in Christianity no less than any other religion. This is completely congruous with Christian anthropology: man is essentially capable of creatively transcending his immediate and literal circumstances, to find ways of understanding and interpreting the world. Jesus himself perceived the value of the story-form in communicating meaning — hence his use of parables. This form of creativity, observes Tolkien, 'remains a human right: we make in our measure and in our derivative mode, because we are made: and not only made, but made in the image and likeness of a Maker.'[16]

Let us take the Apostles' Creed for instance. In the words 'he was crucified, suffered death and was buried,' we have a statement of historically verifiable fact. Juxtaposed with such a statement however, there is an altogether different kind of language which is imagistic and non-empirical,

(14)   Teleketics E.M.I. (London)
(15)   HALBFAS op. cit. p. 203
(16)   TOLKIEN, J.R.R. *Tree and Leaf* (Unwin, 1964) p. 50

'. . . on the third day he rose again. . .he ascended into heaven and is seated at the right hand of the Father.' This calls for quite a different sort of response. It is not that the first is true and acceptable and the second false, but that the essence of the Christian Gospel is of such richness that images and symbolic expressions must be sought which are ever more transparent of a deep, abiding and really experienced reality — the presence of the Spirit in life and history. The Scripture writers themselves knew all there was to be known about poetry, imagination, symbolism and literary devices in order to express their awareness of the continued presence of Christ. (Cf. Ch. 5.10) Christian joy resides in this meeting and fusion of the two worlds of myth and history. 'Redeemed Man is still man. Story, fantasy, still go on, and should go on. The Evangelium has not abrogated legends; it has hallowed them, expecially the "happy ending." The Christian has still to work, with mind as well as body, to suffer, hope and die; but he may now perceive that all his bents and faculties have a purpose, which can be redeemed. So great is the bounty with which he has been treated that he may now, perhaps, fairly dare to guess that in Fantasy he may actually assist in the effoliation and multiple enrichment of creation. All tales may come true; and yet, at the last, redeemed, they may be as like and as unlike the forms that we give them as Man, finally redeemed, will be like and unlike the fallen that we know.'[17] Rollo May makes the assertion that the use of symbol and myth fulfils an integrative function as man's attempt to overcome the dichotomy between subjective experience and objective reality. In this process new meaning is revealed.[18]

Stories then can be a unique and powerful vehicle of meaning. But the distinction between a good and bad story must be made by discerning the quality of its language and style. The mark of a good story is that it *involves* the listener in its world, enables him to get inside its reality.[19] Every sentence should have a life of its own which potentially 'speaks' to the child and touches on his experiences. Halbfas suggests that a good story should leave us with the feeling that 'life is like that,' man and his world are like that; not necessarily in any literal sense, but in possessing that mark of transparency which gives depth and insight to the listener's own interpretation of reality. Thus new possibilities are opened up for the child. So-called 'realistic' literature which simply presents a photograph or mirror image of the world does not always point us towards meaning.

(17)   Ibid. p. 63
(18)   ROLLO MAY *The Courage to Create* (Collins, 1976)
(19)   Cf. LEWIS, C.S. *The seven Narnia Books* (Puffin)

Consequently, neutral and factual accounts of the life of a saintly figure, or even a story which accurately reflects a child's own life-situation may frequently be less useful as a vehicle of meaning than good science fiction or fantasies about worlds where animals talk and toys come to life.[20] Sallie TeSelle observes that 'in a sense a good story, a true story, is "true to" the structure of human experience. It is also, of course, a deformation of that experience, the placement of that story in a new context, and it is this that makes for the creativity of art, its novelty, moving us beyond where we are.'[21]

Assuredly, the story-teller or writer 'must have a vital love of reality,'[22] but it is precisely this love which should carry him with vision towards and beyond the boundaries of the observable world and man's known achievements into new possible worlds and an ever deeper discovery of the potential of human existence. The limits of the actual and the possible, the mundane and the transcendent, are integrated in the story-form in a way exactly consonant with what man already is and what he is continually striving, in his creativity, to become.

3.3   Knowledge, Meaning and Experience

The Incarnational approach is concerned with the child as a whole person, — feelings, reason and imagination. This is why we must now investigate the possibility of an integrated principle for defining the concept of meaning. This might be done by testing the 'realms of meaning' and 'forms of knowledge' debate against actual human experience. For on the experiential plane, knowledge and meaning are integrated at varying levels and to varying degrees. Conceptual distinctions serve to clarify the area for philosophical analysis, but there is no logical necessity to maintain that such distinctions are actual in existential terms. For the child involved in the continuous adventure of learning and the quest for meaning, everything both cognitive and affective is potentially revelatory. Each age and stage

---

(20)   Cf. HALBFAS op. cit., pp. 121–2 (story of St. Damian) RUDOLF STEINER *The Kingdom of Childhood* (Rudolf Steiner Press, 1964) p. 71–2 (story of the little violet) WILLIAMS, M. *The Velveteen Rabbit* (Corgi-Carousel, 1978) TED HUGHES *The Iron Man* (Faber & Faber, 1968) MAURICE SENDAK *Where The Wild Things Are* (Bodley Head, 1963) ANTOINE de SAINT-EXUPERY *The Little Prince* (Puffin, 1962)
(21)   SALLIE TESELLE *Speaking in Parables* (SCM, 1975) p. 138
(22)   HALBFAS op. cit. p. 121

contains that mystery of awareness, growth, discovery and love as the child explores his own unique possibilities and pieces together his fragmentary experience of life. (Cf. Ch. 5.5)

Our starting-point must be to take the meaning/knowledge relation and examine it not from two different sets of assumptions, but from a single premise: meaning is knowledge taken up with wisdom and interiorised with love. This premise derives from an incarnational understanding of man himself, which holds any form of dualistic anthropology to be a contradiction of the divine image in which man is lovingly created. 'The reciprocity and inner union of knowledge and love reflect not only the primordial ground of man's unity, but the concrete history of his personal unity as well. . . . As a man loves more truly, in a way proper to the object of his love, his knowledge becomes more profound.'[23] Cognition remains detached from humanity unless taken up by the subject into himself — and interpreted wisely. 'Subjectivity,' Maritain asserts, 'this essentially dynamic, living and open centre, both receives and gives. It receives through the intellect, by superexisting in knowledge. It gives through the will, by superexisting in love.'[24] There can thus be diverse levels of what might be termed 'cognitive meaning' from the briefest insight to the most profound awareness or expertise, the entire spectrum underpinned by what Frankl refers to as man's innate desire to actualise as many aspects of his mysterious potential as possible — the 'will-to-meaning.' 'Men can give meaning to their lives by realising what I call creative values, by achieving tasks. But they can also give meaning to their lives by realising experiential values, by experiencing the Good, the True, and the Beautiful, or by knowing one single human being in all his uniqueness. And to experience one human being as unique means to love him.'[25]

Human relationship is perhaps the example par excellence of this fundamental 'will-to-meaning.' Claiming that the idea of love at first sight is by no means necessarily neurotic or immature, Rollo May points out that what we 'know' at the experiential level must nevertheless take time to penetrate through to other conscious and conceptual levels. 'The suddenly beloved elicits a composite image from our experiences in our past or in our dreams of our future; we spontaneously recognise him or her in relation

---

(23) GABRIEL MORAN *Theology of Revelation* (Herder & Herder, 1966), pp. 156–7

(24) JACQUES MARITAIN *Human Knowledge and Metaphysics*, p. 91

(25) FRANKL op. cit., p. 12

to our personal "style of life" which we form and carry with us all our lives and which becomes clearer the more fully we know ourselves. But it takes time for the integrating process to take place, time for eros to be interwoven with the multitude of memories, hopes, fears, aims, ad infinitum which form the pattern we recognise as ourselves.'[26]

This tension between subjectivity and other-relatedness, between I and Thou, between individual and community, between what we are and what we can become, lies at the root of Rahner's theological anthropology. Man's 'obediential potency,' the divine spark within, moves him continually beyond himself in a dialectical process of loving and knowing: the more he transcends himself and the more he loves, then the deeper his self-discovery and the more intensely human becomes his apprehension of existence. 'Personal knowledge,' observes Moran, 'is a rising toward unity and at the same time a regrounding of knowledge and love in the unity from which they originally sprang.'[27]

For the child too the quest for integration of self and experience is motivated by the 'will-to-meaning', which involves all dimensions of factual knowledge, feelings, emotions and intuitive awareness. The boy in the film *Kes* struggled to a meaningful synthesis through all these levels, his love for the kestrel providing him for the first time with a reason for learning, a capacity for self-expression, a discovery of natural wonder, and appreciation.[28] Similarly, the young hero of *Storm Boy* learns of love, life and death through his attachment to a pelican, and is helped towards a painful discovery of overall meaning by a wise aboriginal friend.[29] Dibs too moves gradually through his twilight world of self-refusal and alienation, emerging courageously into full personhood and community consciousness. After a paticularly tough session of role-play in which Dibs successfully copes with his own intropunitive reactions, he writes a letter to himself:

> 'Dear Dibs,
>
> I washed the tea set and I closed the drain. I had a party. Children were there.
>
> With love,
> Me.

(26)   ROLLO MAY *Love and Will* (Fontana, 1972) p. 238
(27)   MORAN op. cit., p. 159
(28)   BARRY HINES *A Kestrel for a Knave* (Pergamon, 1969)
(29)   COLIN THIELE *Storm Boy* (BBC Publications, 1978)

. . . He pulled the calendar toward him and leafed through it. He turned to the current day. "This is today," he said. "I will put a big X on it. . . . It is my most important day," he said quite seriously. "I know".'[30]

To discover meaning is to discover love. It is true to say, however clichéd, that unless there is love in one's life in one form or another, then very little else makes sense. This is because the capacity to love is essential to man's nature and must necessarily find its realisation existentially. In an authentically loving act knowledge is transformed; in a fully human recognition of love, what we know and what we feel are integrated into meaningful patterns which determine our self-awareness and our humanity. 'Between love and intelligence there can be no real divorce. Such a divorce is apparently consummated only when intelligence is degraded or, if I may be allowed to use the expression, becomes merely cerebral. . . . But this we must assert, and as forcibly as possible: where love on one side, where intelligence on the other, reach their highest expression, they cannot fail to meet.'[31] Marcel's reference here to 'intelligence' may be understood as a concept relating to cognition, i.e. that which hitherto in this discussion we have termed 'knowledge'.

The fullest expression of integration may be seen in Christ himself. In his life, death and resurrection he established a pattern of meaning which for the Christian is the key to the whole strange business of human existence, with all its contradictions and affirmations, its pain and its joy. In the man Jesus there coheres the twofold movement of revelation: the initiative of God towards man in a gift of love, and the perfect and free response of man's love in return. (Cf. Ch. 1.4) Jesus was no superman. His self-discovery was a painful process of growth, involving hunger, disappointment, exhaustion and also fearful realisations as is illustrated by the Gethsemane passage of Scripture. At every stage he must have had to reconcile his factual awareness of danger and consequences to himself with the abiding love at his centre, which in spite of everything motivated him towards Calvary and through death to resurrection. The Incarnation reveals and illuminates the meaning of our experience: the precariousness and tragedy of love; its power to transform and promote growth; the mysterious death-character of much that we live through; the ultimate fullness of life which can emerge from suffering. And this takes place in all kinds of ways throughout our personal history, from infancy to old age. Incarnation

---

(30) VIRGINIA AXLINE *Dibs: In Search of Self* (Pelican, 1971) pp. 118, 120
(31) GABRIEL MARCEL *Men Against Humanity* (London, 1952) p. 7

has revealed that humanity is living God's life and therefore experience cannot essentially be divided up into categories of what we know, what we love and what things mean. 'Christianity is the announcement that there is an ultimate depth (or height) of human existence where knowing and decision, truth and goodness, are no longer separable. At that point of existence man is related to God who is the presupposition of human freedom and intentionality and at the same time their fulfilment.'[32] We are created whole and the total thrust of our being is towards the actualisation of that wholeness; to break out of the limitations imposed upon us by time and space and to allow the 'hidden self' to develop and grow strong.

Religious education based on the Incarnational approach takes this view of man as fundamental to the structure of the curriculum and as determining all its objectives. The promotion of integrated self-realisation in the child and assisting a deepening awareness of community, should be the primary aims reflected in both content and methods. As one who is both loving and knowing the child apprehends meaning in and through his daily experiences; analyse his apprehension into essentially different activities and we not only contradict his nature, but we run the risk too of inhibiting his growth towards fullness of humanity.

---

(32)   MORAN op. cit. p. 159

Chapter Four
Experience as 'Content' in Education

4.1 The Contribution of Kevin Nichols

Perhaps the most significant recent work in the field of Catholic education in this country is Kevin Nichols' book entitled *Cornerstone*.[1] This is a valuable guideline for R.E. teachers and the promised sequels will, assuredly be most useful. Yet Mgr. Nichols would himself probably concur that there can never really be a final word on the subject of the R.E. curriculum; it is a field within which our understanding must constantly deepen and develop. It will be useful therefore, to examine some of the central theses of the book in the light of an Incarnational approach.

Nichols distinguishes two main strands in contemporary theology of revelation. In the first place, an understanding of revelation as the transmission of a 'deposit of faith', an objective body of knowledge located in the propositions of scripture and doctrine. This view, he suggests, can be rescued from remaining static and extrinsic by a theory of development based on the theology of a living tradition, which is continually evolving, within history. In educational terms this dynamic element provides the corrective to a purely objective approach in the teaching of religion.

In the second place, there is a view of revelation which stresses the subjective aspect, the personal apprehension of revelation within the context of daily living. 'It speaks of "revelatory communion". God speaks to the individual in and through his own experience. That experience includes the teachings of Scripture and the Church, but these play a subsidiary role. In the foreground stands the individual's subjective relationship with God and this is something which he discovers in the whole of his human experience.'[2] This subjective view, Nichols observes, is far too broad and fits perhaps too neatly into current educational theory. A curriculum based on this interpretation emphasises experience and discovery rather than doctrinal knowledge, and its expressions often 'seem to add up to humanism with a vague aura of divinity.'

We wish to make two important points here. First, it might be sugges-

---

(1)   KEVIN NICHOLS *Cornerstone* (St. Pauls, 1978)
(2)   Ibid. p. 65

ted that the experiential understanding of revelation needs a more adequate examination in order to avoid misconceptions. One of the most outstanding exponents of this view is Gabriel Moran to whom Nichols appears to give short shrift. Moran would strenuously contest the connotations of 'privacy' attaching to the term 'subjective'. Indeed, in the quotation cited by Nichols and elsewhere Moran speaks very definitely of the importance of community and the intrinsically relational character of revelation. 'Revelation is what happens between persons and exists only as a personal reality. If there is revelation anywhere in the Church today, it can only be in the conscious experience of the people.'[3] Moreover, this view is well authenticated in present-day Catholic philosophy. Bernard Lonergan suggests that there has been a tendency to think of truth 'as so objective as to get along without minds,' which constitute the actual conditions of its emergence and existence. 'The same insistence on objective truth and the same neglect of its subjective conditions informed the old catechetics, which the new catechetics is replacing.' 'The fruit of truth must grow and mature on the tree of the subject, before it can be plucked and placed in its absolute realm.'[4] This does not contradict a theology of living tradition, but emphasises more strongly that the community which creates such a tradition consists in subjects or persons, each of whom possess individual worth which is decisive for the community — no people, no community. If education and catechesis is our field, then it is experiential language into which the concept of 'living tradition' must be translated.

The second point we wish to make here concerns the function and aims of 'the teachings of Scripture and the Church' in an experience-based curriculum. This will be properly developed in the next two sections of the present chapter, but should be introduced briefly here. Nichols fears that the experiential approach renders the role of Scripture and doctrine a subsidiary one. True he observes, some human experiences have 'an implicit connnection with the truths of faith,'[5] but as such a curriculum which explores these experiences constitutes a 'precatechesis' in the faith; the ground may be prepared by this means for explicitly religious themes. 'An experience-based curriculum is a precatechetical laying down of the human groundwork on which explicit religion can be built in later life.' This approach in essence divorces the ordinary living experience of chil-

---

(3)   MORAN *Theology of Revelation* p.20
(4)   BERNARD LONERGAN *The Subject* (Aquinas Lectures Series, 1968) pp. 5, 4
(5)   NICHOLS op. cit. p. 105

dren from their so-called religious experience; religious content seems to consist in something tacked on at the end of experience. From an Incarnational standpoint we would contend that this cannot be done without, in the proper sense of the word, dis-integrating the child. Scripture and doctrine, so far from being diminished in the Incarnational approach to R.E., are the essential means of highlighting the child's normal experience of life. The Incarnation of Christ has established once and for all that the the totality of human experience is deeply significant in terms of man's salvation. The function of explicitly religious content therefore, is to illuminate and bring to a level of awareness in the child the full value and meaning of all his experiences.

We have confined our comments to what appear to be two of Nichols's most important theses. First, that the subjective view distorts the concept of revelation by making human experience paramount; second, that an experience-based curriculum is a preparation for the specifically religious content of Scripture and doctrine. Each thesis must be adequately answered by the Incarnational approach and the remainder of this chapter is an attempt to expand on the foregoing comments within a curriculum framework which we have called the dialectical model.

A final remark needs to be made about *Cornerstone*. One of the most difficult problems in theology has always been in defining the exact relationship between Christian revelation and the recognised fact that in some way 'all creation speaks of God.' Nichols suggests that the subjective view of revelation makes the link in the following way: 'Central to the Christian belief are the ideas of the freedom and dignity of man, the sacredness of human relations, the universality of grace. Therefore, central to christian belief is a universal concept of revelation. Lift up the stone marked "open-ended R.E." and you find another stone marked "The Christian doctrine of man".' Lift up that stone and you will find another marked "The Christian doctrine of God".'[6] But is the link in fact made in this way? While any attempt to explain who it is established must remain relatively inadequate, the 'three stones' theory as we shall call it is particularly unsatisfactory for the Incarnational approach. Its construction of reality is planar and compartmentalised, founded principally on doctrinal rather than experiential categories. Some way to a solution might be gained if we are prepared to venture into the very area which Nichols feels at this stage should be avoided, namely 'the never-ending theological problem': the

---

(6)   Ibid. p. 65

relation between nature and grace.[7] It could be that to avoid attending to this relation is to bypass the centre of the discussion. For that reason much of the first part of this book is concerned with this question, on which current theological thinking is so significant that it is worth restating briefly.

Man is a creature of unlimited possibilities; he is by nature open to the infinite. By very virtue of being created by God man is graced as is all of creation. He lives by the gift of divinity, the 'divine spark', which makes him the living image of his creator. Man possesses therefore an innate caacity for self-trancendence, for movement towards another, for community, for love. He has a real capacity to listen, receive, respond, to create, imagine and to devise symbols for his own understanding of himself and his world. The 'supernatural,' far from being a superimposed perfection projected vertically into the horizontal plane of the 'natural,' is rather the all-pervasive 'factor' that makes man who he is in all his potential for loving and giving. This is the essence of humanity itself. On this basis, 'pure nature' is what many theologians term a 'limit concept' – a possibility which must be borne always in mind, to appreciate and remember that the gift *is* a gift.[8] It is not a concept that has any real historical content. The distinction between nature and grace, when we use it, serves a theological purpose not an historical or chronological one.

The implications of this for the Incarnational approach are far-reaching. The whole of creation is seen as Incarnation writ large. Nothing and no-one is beyond the absolute presence of the Risen Christ. All that men know and experience, in potency and in actuality, is intrinsically related to the movement towards full humanity for which Christ is our paradigm. Our doctrines of God and man are forever inextricably linked in the fact of the Incarnation.[9] In this light the 'three stones' theory appears quite inadequate. It becomes less clear how there can be a separation of God and man in the actual living experience of people, and 'open-ended R.E.' becomes an all-ebracing exploration into man's own being in the context of the incarnate God, Christ. '. . . "God is with us" in, through, under, and for our human, historical, temporal world. In such a perspective, the doctrines of creation and redemption take on a new meaning – *God*

---

(7) Ibid. p. 66
(8) Both K. Rahner and J. L. Segundo have developed the debate in these terms.
(9) PAUL VAN BUREN *Theological Explorations* (SCM, 1968) p. 181

himself formed the world and re-forms it, the world was never without his power and presence, it was never alone.'[10]

Cornerstone is indeed an extremely useful book, but we suggest that there are many areas which require developing in order to arrive at an overall curriculum design for R.E. It is to this task of development that we now turn.

4.2 Two Dimensions of Awareness in Experience

Our understanding of the nature of human experience may be deepened by a reinterpretation of mystery in Christian theology. Traditionally mystery has been regarded largely as a property attaching to a doctrinal statement; an essential characteristic of the Trinity for instance, which renders it provisionally incomprehensible to human reason. There is indeed a strange inadequacy about our attempts to formulate the vastness of the Christian reality, yet if revelation is capable of being experienced there must certainly be something of the intrinsic quality of mystery about human experience itself to which a purely objective interpretation hardly does justice. 'Grace,' says Rahner, 'enfolds man, the sinner and the unbeliever too, as his very sphere of existence which he can never escape from.'[11] The mystery of divine life not only encompasses the whole of mankind, but also endows the human race with the very impetus and potential for delving more and more deeply into the possibilities of its humanity.

Mystery is not an eternal riddle, or something we can never know about until life after death; nor is it a truth only partially revealed. It is the natural unity which lies at the centre of man, the corrective to his fragmentedness. The Incarnation of Christ reveals that the realisation of mystery is a living possibility for all human beings, to be apprehended above all in love. It is the foundation of our being, the 'pulse' of creation permeating all life. Prior to all duality and conceptualisation mystery is that which motivates man towards the discovery, recognition and expression of love and meaning; that which makes music, poetry, art, invention and all forms of creation and self-giving possible. It is not a puzzle to be solved but, as Moran puts it, 'an inexhaustible depth of meaning' which leads us to ever richer syntheses of all that we know and experience.

---

(10) SALLIE TESELLE *Speaking in Parables* p. 6
(11) KARL RAHNER *Nature and Grace* (Sheed & Ward, 1968) p. 32

The business of education should first and foremost concern itself with encouraging in young people the sensitive apprehension of the truly mysterious character of their experience. It cannot be the case, as Kevin Nichols might argue, that this experience is a distinctive 'point of entry' towards the mysteries of faith, alongside the other 'points of entry' — namely Scripture, doctrine and liturgy. Experience should not be considered an additional 'content-area' for R.E. in this manner. Rather, it constitutes the existential condition for all content whatsoever, whether in the formulations of Scripture and doctrine or in liturgical celebration. The continually graced character of human experience, with all its sufferings, joys, encounters and disappointments, is essentially revelatory; for in it reside the capacity to love and the potency for all meaning. 'The glory of God is a man fully alive, and the life of man is the vision of God.' This must be so if the reality of the Incarnation of Christ is not to be reduced to an empty concept.

The Incarnational approach then must allow positive revelatory value to overall human experience. But it must ensure that specific and decisive significance is attributed to the historical revelation of Christianity. We suggest that the traditional distinction between general (or universal) and special (or specific) revelation could prove extremely useful here. Properly understood this is not an essential distinction between two different kinds of revelation, but a distinction between two dimensions of awareness within one and the same context of human experience. (Cf. Figure 3)

'Knowledge of God', observes Jacques Maritain, 'is first and foremost a natural fruit of the intuition of existence.'[12] Man possesses the potential to know God because man himself is created and exists. This statement of so-called 'natural theology' must for the Christian be interpreted in the light of the Incarnation. Christ has given flesh to the bones of philosophy. 'Christianity places man in a relationship which leaves far behind the services of a metaphysical knowledge of God and makes this practically superfluous. Therefore, theological metaphysics actually died the day Christ was born.'[13] We can no longer say that we do not and cannot know the transcendent God. Christ is God become man, the transcendent within the immanent. To suggest that we cannot know God completely in him is heresy. If God is truly love, then he has emptied himself totally in

---

(12)   JACQUES MARITAIN *Human Knowledge and Metaphysics* p. 90
(13)   HANS URS VON BALTHASAR *Meeting God in Today's World* (Concilium VI/1, 1965) pp. 16–17

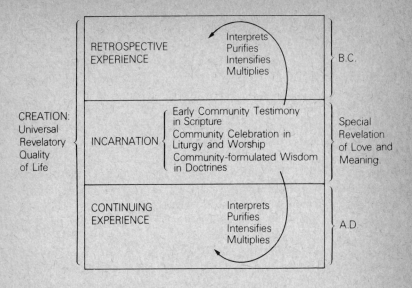

Figure 3: History of God in the World

Christ; the actual humanity of Christ must be the living reality of his divinity. If the person of Christ does not contain and manifest all that God is in himself and for men, then we are most certainly barking up the wrong tree for our religious beliefs — we might well belong to any other faith-community. The point is that what is traditionally termed 'natural theology' does not strictly concern that which man can know of God by means of *unaided* reason, for all creation is graced with divinity; from the start the Spirit of Christ enlivens all man's orientations towards good. It is indeed a concept by which we distinguish Christian awareness from the overall human apprehension of truth and goodness, but it has no factual content as such.

Where we frequently go astray is in the contention that our Christian awareness is an altogether different experience, both qualitatively and with regard to the constituent elements of our humanity which are 'experience-able.' It is almost as if the Christian's experience of love were something different in quality and even derived from a different source, from the love of someone belonging to another faith-community or none! This strange duality arises from a misunderstanding of the specificity of Christianity.

Christian awareness pertains not to a set of self-justifying truths which make sense and function principally in terms of those who are conscious of them. Christian awareness is rather the awareness of the fact that 'wherever love is, God is.' Alan Richardson emphasises that the special revelation of Christianity is 'no mere addition to general revelation, as revealed knowledge was formerly thought to be an addition to natural knowledge; it is rather the means by which the truths given in general revelation can be adequately apprehended and known to be true.'[14] Christian revelation is natural revelation come to full awareness of itself. Whatever is known of God prior to the Christian revelation is fulfilled, not in the sense of being essentially changed but in the specific consciousness of the significance of that knowledge for human existence in the world. Incarnation is the fulfilment of natural theology — the 'God of the philosophers' is shown to be 'the God of Abraham, Isaac and Jacob' in the flesh and blood revelation of the man, Jesus Christ.

The distinction then, lies not between 'mere' human experience on the one hand and revelation on the other, but in the dimensions of awareness relating to one and the same reality; namely, that as a matter of fact all life, all experience, all knowledge is encompassed by the Spirit of Christ — from the moment of creation when the Word of life was first uttered, and from the dawn of the Resurrection when the conversation was fulfilled. This is the real significance of the Christian consciousness. 'We may say,' observes W. H. Vanstone, 'that Christ, the Incarnate Word, discloses to us, at the climax of His life, what word it was that God spoke when "He commanded and they created." It was no light or idle word but the Word of love.'[15] The consciousness of the Christian community is the consciousness of those who *know* that 'from the power of Christ's continuing humanity, all that is human has become revelational of God.'[16]

This view of the intrinsic relation between experience and revelation has important implications for educational theory. We no longer see the child's experience of life as being one of several 'content-areas' which contribute to the objective make-up of R.E. The so-called 'natural knowledge' of the child becomes the *sine qua non* of the entire process, the original gift of vision which is further enlightened and deepened by what

---

(14)   ALAN RICHARDSON *Christian Apologetics* (SCM, 1974) p. 134
(15)   W. H. VANSTONE *Love's Endeavour, Love's Expense* (1978) p. 70
(16)   MORAN op. cit. p. 130

we specifically offer the child by way of Scripture, doctrine, liturgy and all other media employed to illuminate the total spectrum of his experience.

Wide repercussions which this approach has on the structure of the curriculum cannot be understated. The following section offers a suggested design for the interrelationship of the various curricular components. However, a note should be made first of all regarding an activity of great importance in any Church school community – the activity of worship. This has been a contentious issue for some time[17] in terms of the place of school assemblies, liturgical services and other explicit forms of corporate worship. The Incarnational approach seeks to avoid an essential devaluation of human experience in the economy of salvation. We have seen that on this basis the whole experiential capacity of man is intrinsically related to the proper nature of revelation. Within this interpretation the concept of worship undergoes expansion. Worship takes its roots not primarily from liturgical or formal devotion, but from a wider incarnational sphere which touches every area of our daily life. It is the act we make whenever love extends beyond ourselves; when we perceive the depth and value and meaning of all the resources at our fingertips, of the mystery of creation and human relationships, of the endless variety of the animal kingdom, of the wonder of invention, research and discovery, of the beauty of landscapes, art, poetry and music.

'The world is charged with the grandeur of God . . .

> Because the Holy Ghost over the bent
> World broods with warm breast and with ah! bright wings.'[18]

Praise, thanksgiving, glorifying and celebration are all actions arising from real experiences which evoke in us the apprehension that there is a deep reality about our world, the meaning of which has been brilliantly highlighted in Christ. All men have a natural capacity for the recognition of the worth of life. C. S. Lewis observes that 'all enjoyment spontaneously overflows into praise'.[19]

In our daily experience the world rings with praise. Lovers praise the beloved as is illustrated in the great love poems of literature:

> 'Shall I compare thee to a summer's day?
> Thou art more lovely and more temperate . . .'[20]

---

(17) Cf. JOHN HULL *School Worship: An Obituary?* (SCM, 1975)

(18) HOPKINS, G.M. *God's Grandeur*

(19) C. S. LEWIS *Reflections on the Psalms* (Fontana, 1960) p. 80

(20) SHAKESPEARE *Sonnet XVIII*

The poet praises too the richness of nature, by employing his particular gift as the vehicle for the expression of worship, of autumn Keats writes with evident sensuous enjoyment:

> 'Season of mists and mellow fruitfulness,
> Close bosom friend of the maturing sun;
> Conspiring with him how to load and bless with fruit
> The vines that round the thatch-eaves run . . .'[21]

Walkers praise the countryside; sportsmen praise their favourite sport; we all at some stage find ourselves praising the weather, food, wine, actors, children and so on. Dancers worship in the sheer joy of movement. Worship is the articulation of love and care, the expressed recognition of meaning in our experience.

> 'Glory be to God for dappled things —
> For skies of couple-colour as a brinded cow;
> For rose-moles in all stipple upon trout that swim;
> Fresh-firecoal chestnut-falls; finches' wings;
> Landscape plotted and pieced — fold, fallow, and plough;
> And all trades, their gear and tackle and trim.
> All things counter, original, spare, strange;
> Whatever is fickle, freckled (who knows how?)
> With swift, slow; sweet, sour; adazzle, dim;
> He fathers-forth whose beauty is past change:
> Praise him.'[22]

For Teilhard de Chardin, scientific research and discovery was a genuine form of worship. He perceived all matter to be shot through with divinity. 'Lord Jesus, you who are as gentle as the human heart, as fiery as the forces of nature, as intimate as life itself, you in whom I can melt away and with whom I must have mastery and freedom: I love you as a world, as *this* world which has captivated my heart; — and it is you, I now realise, that my brother-men, even those who do not believe, sense and seek throughout the magic immensities of the cosmos. Lord Jesus, you are the centre towards which all things are moving: if it be possible, make a place for us all in the company of those elect and holy ones whom your loving care has liberated one by one from the chaos of our present existence and who are now being slowly incorporated into you in the unity of the new

(21)   KEATS J. *Ode to Autumn*
(22)   G. M. HOPKINS *Pied Beauty*

earth.'[23] Similarly, all human effort and creativity is an exercise in worship. The worker, the skilled craftsman, the shop assistant, the factory-hand, the coal-miner — all, in their explicit or implicit recognition of the value of work and of the need for rendering mutual support in any human community, are worshipping God and in different ways acknowledging him in their affirmation of human value.

Worship then permeates human life and for this reason it must be not only alive, but actually part and parcel of life itself. It is in the round of human activity that the spirit of the risen Christ is present. Liturgy and formal worship is the explicit celebration deriving from and highlighting every instance of worship which occurs in our daily lives. To liturgical celebration therefore should be brought all human symbols of expression — art, dance, poetry, music, gesture and stillness. (Cf. Ch. 1.6, Ch. 5.11)

The purpose of the foregoing remarks about worship has been to emphasise the radical 'opening up' of experience-based education theory required by the Incarnational approach. Our curriculum must begin and end with this central recognition of the intrinsic sacredness of all the child's experiences and endeavours, however apparently limited. The child is a worshipper in so far as he loves, plays, creates, imagines and attempts always to achieve self-discovery. As Christian educators our concern is to assist the child in developing that dimension of awareness of his relation-ships, games, creations, imaginings, which will focus more fully the signifi-cance of all these experiences for himself and his fellows. In short, to bring the prereflexive dimension of the child's life to self-consciousness in the light of Christ the paradigm of full human awareness.

.3 A Suggested Design for RE

A curriculum model for the Incarnational approach must take human ex-perience to be the fundamental 'content' of R.E. We can no longer justify R.E. programmes solely on the basis of the quantity of pre-packaged data imparted by the teacher and 'learnt' by the pupil, whether it be in terms of 'knowing' their Scripture or 'knowing' their doctrine. Undoubtedly we have moved away from the kind of model which assessed itself purely in relation to the achievement of predetermined objectives. (Cf. Ch. 5.3) But it is less certain that we have established the actual threefold relationship

---

(23)   TEILHARD DE CHARDIN *Hymn of the Universe* (Fontana, 1961) p. 70

obtaining between the pupil, the learning media which stimulate the learning processes, and the meaningful synthesis which should constantly be emerging in the pupil's understanding of himself. It is not easy, particularly at the secondary level, to escape from the idea that the learning process is predominantly a cerebral activity. Yet unless the pupil has wisely interiorised what he knows, with regard to his heart as well as his intellect, then 'knowledge' as such does not become an integrating factor in the pupil's development and self-evaluation. As Charles Davis emphasises: 'Meaning must be felt; it cannot just be registered.'[24]

The Schools Council *Groundplan for the Study of Religion* points out that while some knowledge of the relevant facts about religion is essential, the 'fragmented recognition of the existence of these facts is not enough. For them to have educative value for the student, their significance must be plumbed. In other words, they have to be understood and evaluated.'[25] A body of material which remains on an abstract level both in its content-matter and the method employed for teaching it, cannot find any real and loving response in young people. In a vital sense we become what we know. Unless abstraction can be anchored in ways appropriate to the child's self-awareness, then ultimately he cannot be assisted in his quest for meaning. The Incarnational approach holds that Christian revelation tells us as much about man as it does about God; the curriculum therefore, should deal with the human predicament and the activity of God within it, in a manner which is living and meaningful for young human beings.

The design offered here suggests that the relationship of the curriculum components is structured in a threefold dialectic (Cf. Fig. 4). The curriculum takes its starting-point with the real experience of the child, and its end-point is the living Christian significance of that same experience in terms of the child's own understanding of his humanity and its immense possibilities for love, growth and ever-deeper meaning. Between these two components — the child's life-experience and its ultimate meaning — lies the essential mediating area which includes Scripture, doctrine, liturgy, and all forms of communicating media constituted in the various disciplines of literature, history, dance, drama, music, visual arts and so forth. Bernard Lonergan has this to say about the importance of human experience: 'Existential reflection is at once enlightening and enriching. Not only does

---

(24)   CHARLES DAVIS *Body as Spirit* (Hodder, 1977) p. 10
(25)   *Schools Council Groundplan for the Study of Religion* (London, 1977) p. 18

it touch us intimately and speak to us convincingly but also it is the natural starting-point for fuller reflection of the subject as incarnate, as image and feeling as well as mind and will, as moved by symbol and story, as inter-subjective, as encountering others and becoming "I" to "Thou" to move on to "We" through acquaintance, companionship, collaboration, friendship, love. Then easily we pass into the whole human world founded on meaning, a world of language, art, literature, science, philosophy, history, of family and mores, society and education, state and law, economy and technology. That human world does not come into being or survive without deliber-ation, evaluation, decision, action, without the exercise of freedom and responsibility. It is a world of existential subjects and it objectifies the values that they originate in their creativity and their freedom.'[26] We suggest than that a dialectical model of the curriculum is not only required by the very character of Christian revelation, but also accords with the exigencies of general education theory.

Our design incorporates the analyses of four important thinkers of our time: Jerome Bruner,[27] Philip Phenix,[28] Paul Tillich[29] and Karl Rahner. (See Fig. 4) Bruner's is what we have termed a 'cognitve-significant analy-sis'. He sees the specificity of man to reside in his character as 'knower'; as a creature who learns and discovers meaning by experimentation with and the application of cognitive data to his experience. Our aim is that children develop an understanding of the uniqueness of man in these terms. The history of the race would indicate that there are three chief factors by which man interprets his humanity to himself: the ability to make and use tools; the acquisition of language symbols for communication; and the ca-pacity to structure highly developed forms of socialisation. In *Man: A Course of Study*, Bruner suggests that self-understanding and the gaining of true knowledge which is essentially both intellectually and personally sig-nificant, is mediated by an exploration of history, geography, linguistics, which involves practical experiments in rudimentary tool-making, and sym-bolic communications. Bruner stresses that in the knowledge-acquiring pro-cess we cannot extract the concrete content of the curriculum as though

(26) BERNARD LONERGAN op. cit. p. 30
(27) JEROME BRUNER *Towards a Theory of Instruction* (Harvard University Press 1966)
(28) PHILIP PHENIX *Realms of Meaning* (McGraw-Hill, 1964); *Education and the Worship of God* (Westminster, Philadelphia, 1966)
(29) PAUL TILLICH *Ultimate Concern* (SCM, 1965); *Systematic Theology II* (SCM, 1978)

'content' were a component cognitively separable from its significant dimension. We have often found ourselves doing this in R.E. — evacuating Scripture and doctrine of their true significant value by teaching them in a purely cerebral way. Approaches which persist in this fail to maintain the dialectic between the pupil, the learning process and the emergent understanding. Curriculum, says Bruner, 'is the enterprise par excellence where the line between subject-matter (content) and method (process) grows necessarily indistinct.'[30]

Phenix offers us a 'philosophical-significant analysis'. We have already examined his contribution quite closely in Chapter 3.1. Here we intend to place his analysis within the dialectical design. Man, observes Phenix, is a subject, a personal entity characterised specifically by his continual quest for meaning. In his fragmented experience he seeks to discover wholeness, to create patterns which are meaningful and make sense of his existence. The curriculum should reflect and assist in the maturation of this fundamental trait, by offering the pupil not so much 'compartments' of knowledge, but 'realms of meaning' which help him to expand and unify his experience rather than restrict and divide it. Each of the various disciplines as we have seen, falls within one of these realms; they act as mediating areas between the subject seeking meaning and the ultimate unity or synthesis of experience which is aimed at. Again, too often we empty R.E. of its significant and unifying character by removing Scripture, doctrine and other media from their place in the dialectical framework and compartmentalising the curriculum.

We have called Tillich's analysis 'metaphysical-significant'. For Tillich the specificity of man resides in the ontological structure of his being. (Cf. Ch.1) Man is capable of 'ultimate concern'; he is a creature whose overriding impulse is to conquer negativity, to move towards a new consciousness of who he is. This he does by means of all the various human activities which mediate self-awareness, deepen understanding and point up the full import of what it means to be a human being — the arts, sciences and the innumerable aspects of culture, including philosophy and religion. The terms of Tillich's dialectic are: *form, inhalt and gehalt*. The *form* of things is simply the way things are, the raw material of life through which we experience ourselves. The *inhalt* is the subject-matter which processively represents our experience, for instance in the actual painting of a picture. The *gehalt* is the inner meaning, significance or import of

---

(30)   BRUNER op. cit. p. 72

our experience as expressed for instance in the completed picture. The dialectic of these three elements must be held in tension. We need the painter who sketches on the canvas his skeletal vision of the landscape beyond; we need the structure that begins to emerge from the lines, strokes, colours through which he interprets the landscape; we need the finished work which gathers up and unifies his experience of the landscape, expressing, communicating and intensifying it.

We have already investigated the work of Karl Rahner in some depth (cf. Ch. 1, especially section ii). In the present context his analysis may be understood as 'ontological-significant'. The human person, in his deepest being, is constituted by a fundamental openness to God. Created in the image and likeness of God, man is, in himself, the potentiality for perfect concord with his Maker. In the fabric of self-conscious experience reside the possibilities for self-transcendent meaning, for the realisation of true and full human actuality. This realisation takes place through a gradual process of growth and transformation — a deepening integration which is occasioned by every instance of concrete experience and positive response in man's existence; for example, falling in love, unconditional forgiveness, sacrificing one's own interests, making the effort to understand another and learning to grow in suffering. Through such experiences, and indeed, in the very act of asking questions about life, death and meaning, man participates more and more profoundly in absolute being, thus himself moving towards fuller human maturity — the New Creation — of which the man Jesus Christ is the supreme example and prototype.

The Incarnational approach sees the dialectic of experience, media and meaning to be essential in any curriculum model for R.E. The God who *acts* in and through the prereflexive life of the child, becomes the God who *speaks* through symbols, concepts and judgements, conveying meaning, pattern and coherence to hitherto unexamined experience. Christian revelation, in its uniquely incarnational character, establishes the full value of human experience and therfore actually demands empirical and experience-rooted media for its communication. The illuminating quality of these mediations — particularly Scripture, doctrine and liturgy — specifically points up the potential and meaning of experience. They are the *means* by which the pupil develops experiential insight and understanding in his process of becoming more and more deeply and intensely human and Christlike. Meaning is itself in so far as it continues to be fleshed out and tested against man's experience, and to be celebrated and deepened in his actions, formulations and liturgies which mediate to man the consciousness of who he is. This dialectical model is consistent with an incarnational theology and maintains the fundamental place of the child's experience in the construction of an R.E. curriculum. We should always remember that the child is both a knower and a lover; if the components of the curriculum are so fragmented as to divide the child against himself then he cannot be expected to stand — in a real sense we dis-integrate the child. But precisely where there is an answering echo to what we offer him, which carries him forward to a new synthesis of love and meaning, is precisely where revelation happens for the child. All that we offer him therefore must be constantly checked for authenticity in this respect. (Cf. Ch. 5.4, 11)

Figure 4: **The Dialectical Model**

A Suggested Design for R.E. Based on the Incarnational Approach

J. Bruner Cognitive-significant Analysis	P. Phenix Philosophical-significant Analysis	P. Tillich Metaphysical-significant Analysis	K. Rahner Ontological-significant Analysis	Dialectic of Curricular Components
The Knower	The Subject	Form	Potentia Oboedientialis	What *is* and what happens to the child; the pupil's unexamined, prereflexive feelings and experiences.
Knowledge-acquiring process	Mediating realms	Inhalt	Process of self Transcendence	Actual or empirical media: Scripture, doctrine, liturgy and various modes of communication and interpretation, including interdisciplinary processes.
Knowledge; Understanding	Wholeness; Meaning	Gehalt	The New Creation	Inner meaning or import: experience enlightened by Christian revelation and dynamised by the power of 'new being' which is incarnated and recreated in each pupil's becoming.

PART THREE

A Curriculum Model for
the Incarnational Approach

Chapter Five   Curriculum Notes

5.1   Coherence and Structure in Curriculum Planning

Fragmentation of experience and fragmentation of knowledge result in
poor understanding and much meaninglessness. It is difficult to sustain a
sense of the whole since experience and meanings seldom appear in pure
and simple form. As the Incarnational approach is concerned with making
man's unexamined experience meaningful, much attention must be directed
in future strategy towards providing a comprehensive pattern of fundamental ideas within which all the constituent units and parts of units are
identified and ordered. Attention must be paid too, if this principle of
wholeness is to be maintained, to the pupils' readiness for the various areas
of meaning, the interrelations of these realms of meaning even within one
aspect of Religious Education and the 'intrinsic logical order of the various
kinds of meaning.'

To preserve what might be called the principle of simplicity, and
again in the interests of coherence and wholeness, it seems important that,
given the immense amount of material in the vast numbers of curriculum
guide-lines and syllabus suggestions, the selected units of content be particularly representative of the field of Christianity as a whole. 'The only
effective solution to the surfeit of knowledge,' writes Phenix, 'is a drastic
process of simplification. This aim can be achieved by discovering for each
discipline those seminal or key ideas that provide clues to the entire discipline. If the content of instruction is carefully chosen and organised so as
to emphasize these characteristic features of the disciplines, a relatively
small volume of knowledge may suffice to yield effective understanding of
a far larger body of material.'[1]

Structure has to do with the way in which parts make a whole.
'Grasping the structure of a subject is understanding it in a way that permits many other things to be related to it meaningfully. To learn structure,

---

(1)   GOLDBY, M. et al. (ed.) *Curriculum Design* (Croom Helm: 1975) p. 171

in short, is to learn how things are related.'[2] There are many implications for the R.E. curriculum outline in these considerations. Bruner elaborates his views on the structure of subject-matter by holding that a curriculum should be organised around the fundamental concepts and relationships that give mere factual knowledge and information a deeper and more exciting meaning. The transfer of principles and attitudes becomes possible when learning is centred on key ideas and basic selected conceptual links. For a pupil to be able to recognise the applicability of an idea (or a method of enquiry for that matter) to a new situation, thus continually broadening and deepening his understanding and relevant knowledge, he must have clearly in mind the general nature and fundamental meaning of the phenomenon with which he is dealing. This approach short-circuits the perennial anxiety about how much knowledge should be 'in' the syllabus and about whether or not sufficient content has been 'covered.' Phenix points out that meaning is lost when knowledge is abstruse and only superficially connected, or when it is commonplace and unrelated to experience. The philosophy of the new design for religious education centers on the idea of meaning as the key to distinctively human experience (cf. Ch. 3). The Incarnational approach suggests a basis for the kind of coherence and structure of scope and of sequence that the sections in this chapter point up as desirable and indeed necessary.

Both Bruner and Phenix regard the suggested changes in curriculum structure as enhancing the pupils' sense of excitement about discovery — the discovery of 'regularities of previously unrecognised relations and similarities between ideas, with a resulting sense of self-confidence in one's abilities.'[3] The imagination is brought into play. Creativity and then re-creation is experienced by teacher and pupil. Once the basic ideas, the fundamental principles and the central strategies and modes of enquiry are mastered then a sense of the extraordinary and suprising is imparted and learning becomes a continuous adventure. Such an approach 'generates habits of thought that enable the student to respond to rapid changes in knowledge and belief with zest instead of dismay and to experience joy in understanding rather than the dead weight of ideas to be absorbed and stored.'[4] Nowhere more than in religious education would such a possibility be welcomed. Among some other implications of the new curriculum

---

(2)   ibid. p. 445
(3)   ibid. p. 171
(4)   ibid. p. 172

structure for education in general, and for the proposed R.E. design in particular, the following then may be numbered:-

i)   a subject is made more comprehensible in depth by an initial introduction to and understanding of the key concepts and fundamental ideas of that subject;

ii)   knowledge is made more memorable when situated within a framework of basic and personal usefulness and meaning where the pupil is seen in the totality of his personality. 'Perhaps the most basic thing that can be said about human memory, after a century of intensive research, is that unless detail is placed into a structured pattern, it is rapidly forgotten. Detailed material is conserved in memory by the use of simplified ways of representing it. These simplified representations have what may be called a 'regenerative character'[5];

iii) an emphasis on structure and principles in teaching, by its constant reference to basic and central ideas and concepts, narrows the gap between advanced and elementary knowledge.[6] Any approach which facilitates the unbroken progression in the understanding of a subject, as a pupil moves from first to middle to secondary school education, must be given serious consideration and thoroughly researched.

In both its theoretical and practical aspects, the Incarnational approach to a new design in R.E., as outlined in this book, seems to be ideally suited to encompass in its presentation, the philosophical points concerning curriculum structure that have been briefly referred to in this section.

5.2   Objectivity and Rationality in the New Structure

The thesis affirms also the objectivity and rationality of the Incarnational approach. To many it may appear as a subjective exploration into a subjective experience. There is, of course, always this danger, but the view of experience taken in these pages sees it as man's authentic response to reality. Man's feelings and experiences must be submitted to critical reason to test whether his responses to life are valid. Through his depth-experiences a man is in touch with true values — they have, therefore, a cognitive content;

---

(5)   ibid. p. 450
(6)   ibid. p. 451

through them a man is in touch with reality — in this sense they are truly objective.

Just as the philosophical and theological assumptions of the Incarnational approach can be shown to be objective and rational, so too its presentation in an educational setting can be shown to observe all the canons of objectivity and rationality. The three criteria which a subject needs to meet, if its inclusion in the curriculum is to be justified on educational grounds, are, according to Grimmitt:[7]

a) Does this subject incorporate a unique 'mode of thought and awareness' which is 'worthwhile' to man's understanding of himself and his situation?

b) Does this subject serve to widen and deepen the child's cognitive perspective in a unique and valuable way and so contribute to his total development as a person?

c) Can this subject be taught in ways which ensure understanding and actively foster the child's capacity to think for himself?

The Incarnational approach appeals only to those educational criteria for its justification and does not base its claim to a place in the curriculum on either ecclesiastical, 'spiritual', historical, moral or cultural grounds.

We would like to point out here that the currently orthodox notions of initiation, rationality, objectivity and autonomy are often less than adequate as the basic criteria for the total evaluation of an R.E. (or indeed any educational) approach. Kevin Nichols wonders whether a substantially deepened understanding of education could be constructed around wider pivotal ideas. He selects the notions of commitment, search and dialogue which 'chime in a different philosophical register' to the demanding and rigorous style of the English philosphical tradition. 'In giving such a key place to the words commitment, search and dialogue, I am not dismissing the ideas of initiation, rationality and autonomy. I am arguing that they are not on the first level and should not have the first priority. So reason is not rejected in favour of some esoteric alternative. Rationality, like autonomy is assumed into another paradigm. In the interplay of commitment, dialogue and search, it is assumed that rationality in the sense of civilised discourse and the rules of evidence will be honoured. But there are different kinds of rationality and each should have only its appropriate place. In matters of religion we ought to recognise not only the function

---

(7)   GRIMMITT, M. *What Can I do in R.E.?* (Mayhew-McCrimmon: 1973) p. 16

but also the limits of reason'.[8] We mention this suggestion here because it echoes much of the argument pursued in Chapter Three (above).

Even with these last remarks in mind we can see no significant difference in the basic presentation of this approach whether it be pursued with pupils who in some sense or other already belong to the Christian faith or with pupils who do not belong in any sense whatever. There may, however, be a much greater impact on one group rather than the other, just as a project on the topic of Lancaster City, for instance, will have many more emotive and personal overtones for a young Lancastrian than, say, for one who associates the name only with an ageing actor or bomber. Local knowledge, the experience of community, shared pride, personal responsibility, a sense of identity — all these will work towards fleshing the rational appraisal of the life-centre of the City into a new consciousness of personal identity, a deeper self-awarenesss in which loyalty, love, understanding and insight are all affirmed and increased. The objective and rational statements about the realities of life in Lancaster City will be repeatedly internalised by him as he lives and experiences what the other pupil can only reflect on at one step removed, so to speak. Likewise, with the Incarnational approach. It speaks directly to the authentic human experience of all pupils. But the rational presentation of the explanation, purification and multiplication of those experiences in the light of revelation, will carry an intensity of personal meaning (and thus salvation and liberation from fear and ignorance) for the pupil who wishes to be identified as a recipient of that revelation — an intensity of impact that may well not exist for the pupil whose interest in Christianity is that of an observer.

5.3 Curriculum Models and The Incarnational Approach

At the risk of over-simplification, a survey of recent writings on the various structures for educational curricula would seem to identify three main models or designs even though there will inevitably be a large degree of overlap. There will be many significant differences in approach between the supporters of any one curriculum outline mentioned here. In the interests of clarity and in order to avoid misrepresentations, it is necessary that teachers involved in the search for a suitable R.E. curriculum should re-

---

(8)   NICHOLS, K. (ed.) *The Voice of the Hidden Waterfall* (St. Paul's Press: 1980) p. 117

read and revise for themselves some of the very impressive arguments of at least a selected number of the philosophers and educationalists mentioned in this section.

1.   The *'objectives-model'*, sometimes referred to as the 'means-end model', and usually associated with educationalists such as Mager, Tyler and Bloom[9], is based on the achievement of predetermined goals and foreseeable results. The influence of this traditional structure can still be traced in the over-all curricular design of many schools today. Within the R.E. discipline, outlines inherent still in commonly-used Agreed Syllabuses and Catechisms, often associated with a 'confessionalist' approach, rely heavily on this plan. The goal of the 'good Christian' as the end-product of religious education is the deciding factor in the selection of the areas of knowledge and information most suited to that end. The aim is seen in terms of a change in behaviour. There is a specification in advance regarding the final outcome of the change in the pupil. While certain elements of this 'output model' are much criticised today, its continuing presence testifies to its usefulness and strength.

2.   The *'content-model'*, where knowledge is seen in terms of its own intrinsic value, is associated with philosophers of education such as Peters, Hirst and Dearden.[10] The emphasis is on 'content' as a quantifiable and assessable objective. The value of the accumulated knowledge of man is regarded as worthwhile in itself. The selection of educational material is not controlled by the objective of forming or informing the potential end-product of the teaching. Content is selected for its intrinsic worth rather than for its contribution to the achievement of an objective. The keynote of this approach to the curriculum is the emphasis on what 'goes in', and how it is treated, rather than on what 'comes out.' For this reason it is sometimes called the 'input model.'

       No R.E. specialist can afford to ignore the valuable contributions to the advancement of education in this concept of curriculum-design. Indeed most contemporary approaches are strongly influenced by the arguments and reasoning behind this 'content-model.'

       The 'content' of Religion, however, cannot be laid hold upon like other bodies of knowledge such as physics, biology or geography. As a 'form of knowledge' it can scarcely be categorised and defined. The 'con-

---

(9)   cf. BLOOM, B.S. et al. (ed.) *Taxonomy of Educational Objectives (1)* Longman's Green: 1956)
(10)   cf. HOOPER, R. (ed.) *The Curriculum: Content, Design & Development* (Oliver & Boyd: 1972)

tent' of religion is, perhaps even to a greater extent than in the case of other subjects, deeply a part of mystery. The task of the curriculum planner is to find the best ways and means in which the ultimate mystery that all revealed religion is, its 'mysterious reality', can be entered into by teachers and pupils alike.

3.   The *'process-model'* associated with curriculum planners such as Bruner, Dewey and Phenix[11], while respecting the values of the preceding models, emphasises the principles of procedure in sharing and gaining knowledge and wisdom, rather than predetermined goals. The general aim here tends towards the development of the pupils' capacity to search, investigate, acquire understanding and find meaning, judge and assess in an informed way. Understanding and meaning are chosen as an aim because these can never be fully achieved. The goals centre around the process of learning rather than the end-product of the activity. Knowledge is seen as a process rather than a product, as a stage in becoming rather than as an arrival, to be used rather than to be possessed.

This curriculum model reflects not only the nature of knowledge itself but also the nature of the knower and of the knowledge-getting procedure. Subject-matter, method, and persons become fused together in the acquisition of wisdom. A 'spiral' curriculum such as this, as opposed to a 'linear' one, holds that what a child grasps intuitively early on can be cognitively reinforced later. 'Any subject can be taught effectively in some intellectually honest form to any child at any stage of development.'[12] Every subject as we have just seen, has a basic structure of concepts which are acquired in a progressive and cumulative fashion. The function of curriculum designers is to discover this structure and to frame curriculum materials so that pupils engage in 'intellectually honest' learning which is appropriate to their stage of cognitive development but which advances appreciation of the core concepts of the subject, (cf. Ch. 5.1)

The Dialectical Model

The model of curriculum offered here represents an enlargement of model 3 above. It recommends, more emphatically, that between the pupil, the knowledge-acquiring process and the content of the educational programme,

---

(11)   cf. DEWEY, J. *The Child and the Curriculum: School and Society* (Univ. of Chicago Press, 1956)
(12)   BRUNER, J. *Process of Education* (Harvard University Press: 1961)

there obtains a dialectical relation which establishes the full value of each of the component areas. (Cf. Fig. 4)

Curriculum planning is concerned first and foremost, not only with abstract processes, but with persons. It is the person who is always in the process of becoming who, by nature, he already is; of realising his capacity for wholeness. The person is never an educational non-entity. To treat the learning process as separable from the learning subject is hardly satisfactory. Yet the shakiness of much curriculum planning seems to reside in the lack of a secure foundation in *grounded theory*. The ground of all educational theory is the human individual in his existential situation. 'He is a universe unto himself, a microcosm in which the great universe in its entirety can be encompassed through knowledge. And through love he can give himself freely to beings who are to him, as it were, other selves. . . . To say that a man is a person is to say that in the depth of his being he is more a whole than a part and more independent than servile. It is this mystery of our nature which religious thought designates when it says that the person is in the image of God.'[13]

There can be no objectives predetermined in isolation from the human individuals who progress towards fullness (or diminishment) of their humanity and to whom such objectives must always relate. This is particularly true of religious education. The dialectical model, with its overall unity, avoids over-specifying a concrete end-product either in terms of required behaviour or quantity of accumulated knowledge. Growth towards ever-deeper wisdom and sensitivity to the ultimate questions posed by life, proceeds in a person by means of mediating symbols which stimulate understanding, communicate meaning and move the individual towards richer syntheses of his experiences. 'The education process is a continuous process of growth having as its aim at every stage an added capacity of growth.' (Dewey) An indication of appropriate procedures by which the child may interpret the mysterious and frequently confusing phenomena of life and discover for himself patterns of meaning within the context of his own experience, is perhaps the closest we can come to defining the general aim of this model for R.E. Over-specification is destructive of the mystery of humanity, the dialectic is lost and many of the basic assumptions of the Incarnational approach are contradicted.

It has already been pointed out that we cannot give a clear definition of the 'content' of religion in the same way that we are able to define the

---

(13) MARITAIN, J. *Education at the Crossroads* (Yale University Press: 1943) p. 8

content of physics for instance. Whenever we imagine we have grasped the so-called 'content' of Scripture, doctrine or liturgy, we realise that there is always 'something more'; that what we have in fact is a number of areas, albeit essential ones, which function as so many doors to the mystery, as so many lights on human existence. The real content of religion is not primarily an objective body of data; it is life itself. Not life in an abstract, philosophical sense, but *life as it is lived* and experienced by child and adult alike seeking and discovering meaning. The entire enterprise is, as Maritain suggests, not so much one of gaining 'knowledge about' things, but of developing 'knowledge into' the very reality and meaning of things in terms of humankind.

The intrinsic consonance of this curriculum model with an Incarnational approach has been examined closely in Ch. 4, 3. Suffice it to say here that a genuine dialectical tension ensures that the curriculum planner exercises constant vigilance in maintaining an actual and not merely a theorectical interdependence between the child, the mysterious significance to be apprehended and the mediating modes of communication which continually stimulate the cognitive and affective processes. To neglect any one of these three elements is to weaken the curriculum structure.

5.4 A Consideration of Aims

In attempting to clarify the aims and objectives of an R.E. curriculum based on the Incarnational approach, we felt that three principles should be continually borne in mind:

a) the selected aims should satisfy the necessary critieria for a subject to be included on valid educational grounds in the general educational curriculum of any school (cf. Ch. 5.2);

b) the selected aims should reflect a picture of man in his body-spirit totality, whose search for meaning includes, but transcends 'merely' cerebral elements of education (cf. Ch. 3);

c) the selected aims should envisage religion as a distinctive way of interpreting experience and giving meaning to life. There is a uniqueness about the Christian truth-claims here, holding as they do, that revelation makes man more truly conscious of what man already is, that demands much understanding and evaluation on the part of the pupil (cf. Ch. 5.8, 5.10)

Even though 'a change in attitude' is often regarded as a justifiable aim only within an evangelical or apostolic catechetical system devoted chiefly to 'nurture', many phenomenologists today can accept as legitimate a number of objectives in religious education which are couched in terms of attitude-change. Among such objectives the authors of *A Groundplan for the Study of Religion* number the following: the promotion of greater sensitivity in areas of experience relevant to the field of religion; of a willingness to examine the nature and grounds of one's own belief; an acceptance of the necessity for applying intelligence to the area of one's own religion; the willingness, when forming one's attitudes, to take into account the wide variety of current attempts to 'make sense of the human condition' without abandoning one's commitment to one's own vision of truth; the stimulation of each pupil's search for a meaningful patterning of his life which is both ethical and consonant with reason, and finally, an acceptance of the possibility that one's own position needs continual reassessment.[14]

Every educationist and teacher has a vision of what he hopes will be achieved as a result of his efforts. The science teacher aims at a knowledge and understanding of the concepts and coherence of the physical world; at developing the skills of practical experiment and encouraging attitudes of value towards the observable phenomena of the universe. Specified knowledge, skills and attitudes of this kind are far more difficult to pin-point for the Christian R.E. teacher. Yet in this area the problem of *overall aim* becomes even more fundamental. As Phenix observes, the realm of religion tries to see some comprehensive, overarching meaning which includes science, art, morality and the rest, but reaches somehow beyond their partial syntheses to the mysteriously cosmic character of man, that feature which enables him to experience all these realms as aspects of a greater whole. '(Religion) tries to find a tested framework in which men and women can come to terms, not only with the mysteries of suffering and sense of "sin", the brevity of human life and its seeming futility, but also with experiences of beauty, joy in living and loving relationships.'[15]

Rudolf Steiner, founder of the Waldorf school, poses the question in the following way: 'How can we bring to revelation in a man what lies god-given within his nature?' The Incarnational approach addresses itself to the

(14)   SCHOOLS COUNCIL PROJECT. *A Groundplan for the Study of Religion* (160, Great Portland St., London. 1977) p. 16
(15)   SCHOOLS COUNCIL PROJECT. *Discovering an Approach* (Macmillan Education: 1977) p. 10

task of providing an educationally honest and theologically sound framework for the achievement of the aim implicit here.

Clearly, the aim is not to mould the child into hard and fast preconceived patterns of behaviour, ethical or intellectual; neither is it to induce Christian 'belief' by manipulating the emotions and inhibiting autonomous reasoning processes. Indoctrination of this type is inadmissible. The education of man is a human awakening. Therefore, the *aim* of education is the unfolding or realisation of the individual's own essence; it is 'to guide man in the evolving dynamism through which he shapes himself as a human person'.[16]

Too often education is referred to only in terms of particular discipline — physics, literature, geography, chemistry and so on. These are convenient and indeed necessary compartments by which we distinguish the categories and concepts properly applied to the various aspects of our fragmented experience. Yet perhaps the more influential factors in the achievement of true education are to be found first of all in the 'extra-educational' sphere of everyday human existence. It is by what happens to him here that the child feels and suffers, and derives the capacity to forge links between his immediate existential experiences and the more formal disciplines of the classroom. This essential interrelatedness of the child's daily experiences of life and the structured subjects of the curriculum is the central concern of the Incarnational approach.

Experience 'is an incommunicable fruit of suffering and memory. . . through which the shaping of man is achieved.'[17] Earliest expressions of awe and wonder indicate that children are deeply sensitive to the dimension of experience long before intellectual understanding emerges. 'Whenever children are being helped towards an awareness of the mystery that bounds our earthly existence, birth, death, the seasonal renewal of nature, and human dependence on the continuation of order and pattern, they are involved in the search for meaning.'[18] Experience then is the ground of all subsequent conceptual interpretation. The claim of the Incarnational approach is that revelation highlights the meaning of experience: the values embodied in the person of Christ reveal man to himself. Incarnation means openness, freedom and true humanity; it is the event which points up the full significance of all that we are and all that we are capable of becoming.

---

(16)   MARITAIN, J. op. cit. p. 9
(17)   ibid. p. 23
(18)   *Discovering an Approach* p. 11

As such the approach demands space for expansion and personal growth, comparable to the unlimited knowing power of man. On this basis, an overall aim for R.E. can never be general in the sense of a precise determination of ends; neither can knowledge, skills and attitudes be understood in a purely cognitive sense. 'If I furnish a child with a concept that is to remain 'correct', a concept which he is to retain throughout his life, that is just as though I bought him a pair of shoes when he was three years old, and each successive year had shoes made of the same size. The child will grow out of them. . . . We furnish the child with ideas which do not grow with him. We give him concepts which are intended to be permanent; we worry him with fixed concepts which are intended to remain unchanged, whereas we should be giving him concepts capable of expansion. We are constantly squeezing the soul into the ideas we give the child.'[19]

The dynamic totality of the child as 'a child of man' – intellect, imagination and emotions – must be respected in the common quest for significance. 'Life as a whole is a unity, and we must not only consider the child but the whole of life; we must look at the whole human being.'[20] Educational aims of autonomy, sensitivity and understanding are ultimately to be sought in certain reactions *unique to a particular person* and his capacities. Our efforts at root are directed at aiding the child to arrive at a proper awareness, realisation and understanding of himself in the world; to organise his multifarious experiences and feelings into a whole which is right for him as a human being among many. In this process, we should retain 'the sense of (the child's) innermost essence and his internal resources, and a sort of sacred and loving attention to his mysterious identity, which is a hidden thing that no techniques can reach.'[21]

5.5   The Kingdom of Childhood and Incarnational Theology

We feel that this piece of work would be incomplete without the brief attempt to express some neglected insights into the nature of childhood. We offer these reflections in the hope that they will contribute to the general arguments for an Incarnational approach to R.E. and that they will be remembered in the future work of the curriculum designers.

---

(19)   STEINER, R. *The Kingdom of Childhood* (Rudolf Steiner Press: 1964) p. 19
(20)   ibid. p. 18
(21)   MARITAIN, J. (op. cit.) p. 9

Two Views of Childhood

There are two views of time as applied to man's growth and development. In the first place there is a kind of linear view of life based on the laws of physical time where the past is lost and the present is a stepping-stone to the future. 'We conceive of our personal life-span as the sum total of a series of phases in life, each of which, as it is exhausted, leads on to the next, the very meaning of which is to disappear into the next, to be a preparation for it, to "exist" for the further stages beyond itself.'[22] We tend to apply this kind of thinking to our view of youth and childhood. The early years are seen as subordinate to the later ones and there is a central preparatory function attached to the initial stages of life. 'And when that for which childhood is a preparation arrives, the — such is our conception — childhood itself disappears.' But the child is more than a sawn-off man, a potential adult, who will one day arrive at his ultimate goal having passed through the stages of his earlier life as definitively and irrevocably as one passes through the stations on a railway journey en route to one's final destination. What happens during the years of childhood cannot, we feel, be always quantified and measured as accurately as some developmental psychologists, such as Jean Piaget, Lawrence Kohlberg and Ronald Goldman, would hold.

The desire to know all is a great temptation. Knowledge ensures control and control is neat, leaving no room for the untidy and the exception. But the child, like the lover and the poet, is a menace on the assembly line. He is outside total evaluation because he is mystery. Mystery confuses the technical expert. 'Piaget's view is that the early stages of life should simply be outgrown, shed like husks; that on the whole they have no permanent value, only a preparatory one. He often describes them as "autistic" (a word we associate with mental illness) or "egocentric" (usually a term of moral condemnation.)[23] Goldman, in turn, is quite clear that young children are 'pre-religious,' having little or no capacity to enter into any kind of religious experience. We will see shortly how the directors of the Religious Experience Research Unit at Oxford have amassed overwhelming evidence to contradict that kind of view.

But there is another kind of time at the heart of man's personal history, less linear and more spiral, less sequential and more concentric. This

---

(22) RAHNER, K. *Theological Investigations, Vol. VIII* (Darton, Longman & Todd: 1971) p.34
(23) NICHOLS, K. *Orientations* (St. Paul's Press: 1980) p. 92

is how Karl Rahner endeavours to introduce the notion of the mystery of childhood and the redemption of time. 'Man is not a thing that is simply pushed through the space-time dimension as though it were only in possession of the transient moment which is called the present. Man is a subject. He possesses himself. He is at all stages capable of taking himself as a whole. And for this reason, in spite of the continuous process of change or the alteration of action and passion in the time to which he is subject, he has before him his time as a whole. . . . By the exercise of his freedom he makes the time alloted to him present to himself as whole, past and future together. He gathers himself up in his completed state. He finds himself. His temporal existence is not something which he brings behind him, but something which he makes present to himself. He does not bring his temporal mode of existence to an end by quitting it, but by compressing it, as it were, and bringing it with him in its totality into his eternity which is his time as summed up and completed. His future is the making present of his own past as freely lived.'[24] There is then an eternal quality about childhood. It is not lived through and cast away like an old coat. It endures as the fullness of the person; we do not lose childhood. Rather we continue to affirm it and in a sense 'we only become the children we were because we gather up time — and in this our childhood too — into our eternity . . . we do not move away from childhood in any definitive sense, but rather more towards the eternity of this childhood, to its definitive and enduring validity in God's sight . . . it is important in itself also, as a stage of man's personal history in which that takes place which can only take place in childhood itself, a field which bears fair flowers and ripe fruits such as can grow in *this* field and in no other, and which will themselves be carried into the storehouses of eternity.'[25]

Childhood is precious and enduring then, not because within it lie the seeds of maturity but because it is full and, in a sense, already mature itself. 'My first remembered experience of the numinous occurred when I was barely three. I recall walking down a little cul-de-sac lane behind our house in Shropshire. The sun was shining, and as I walked along the dusty lane, I became acutely aware of the things around me. I noticed a group of dandelions on my left at the base of the stone wall. Most of them were in full bloom, their golden heads irradiated by the sun, and suddenly I was overcome by an extraordinary feeling of wonder and joy. It was as if I was

---

(24) RAHNER, K. (op. cit.) p. 35
(25) ibid. p. 36

part of the flowers, and stones, and dusty earth. I could feel the dandelions pulsating in the sunlight, and experienced a timeless unity with all life.'[26] Adulthood is not the justification for childhood. The fact that childhood contributes to adolescence and later life is not its only claim to its own intrinsic rightness. It needs no defence because it is already in each moment of its reality, the heart of the man that the child already is. 'There is a sense in which the human being has a perfection proper to his stage of development whatever that stage may be, and in this sense, even a child, unlike a half-formed product of the conveyor belt, is truly finished. The model for human growth must be a process which is perfect and complete in every stage and yet permits further growth and change. . . . Jesus was neither more nor less the Son of God at the age of twenty or thirty than he was at the age of six months. The Word was incarnated fully and perfectly in the child as child, just as in the man as man. And yet the child grew.'[27]

A child grows as a tree grows, wasting nothing, ever more itself as the seasons circle round it, realising its true nature and establishing this nature for ever. The child does not gradually develop adulthood. As his life unfolds he simply realises what he already is. The fullness is there from the beginning; it is not acquired by stages. 'Christianity is aware of the mystery of that beginning which already contains all present within itself, and yet still has to become all; the beginning which is the basis and foundation of all that is yet to come, its horizon and its law, and yet at the same time cannot ever come to its own fullness except in what has still to come in the future.'[28]

The poet too is aware of the realities of spirit, grace and nature united in the single entity of the child. William Wordsworth, for instance, is no stranger to the presence of mystery in childhood.

> Dear Child; dear Girl! that walkest with me here,
> If thou appear untouched by solemn thought,
> Thy nature is not therefore less divine:
> Thou liest in Abraham's bosom all the year,
> And worship'st at the Temple's inner shrine,
> God being with thee when we know it not
>
> *It is a Beauteous Evening*

---

(26)   ROBINSON, E. *The Original Vision* (R.E.R.U.: 1977) p. 49

(27)   BRITISH COUNCIL OF CHURCHES 1976 *The Child in the Church. Arts. 34 & 35*

(28)   RAHNER, K. (op. cit.) p. 38

And Dylan Thomas, with magic words, awakens a half remembered existence, as few others can:

> . . . And I saw in the turning so clearly a child's
> Forgotten mornings when he walked with his mother
> Through the parables
> Of sunlight
> And the legends of the green chapels
> And the twice told fields of infancy
> That his tears burned my cheeks and his heart moved in mine
> *Poem in October*

The Quality of Openness

There are many qualities in the child but the over-riding grace of openness seems to permeate them all. 'Childhood as an inherent factor in our lives must take the form of trust, of openness, of expectation, of readiness to be controlled by another, of interior harmony with the unpredictable forces with which the individual finds himself confronted.'[29] A child possesses freedom in a unique way in that he is not simply the predetermined unfolding of a pre-planned design. For this reason he is receptive and full of hope. Kevin Nichols in his book *Orientations* lists three predominant characteristics of childhood. He mentions, first of all, 'a native sense of wonder — the awareness that things are which precedes the investigation and analysis of what they are.' (p. 93) This sense, he agrees, should persist even into the most sophisticated adult activity, that of scholarship and good theology. As a second trait of childhood he suggests 'the experience of dependence' (p. 94) which he links with the capacity to trust. Dependence should be a permanent part of the human condition. A denial of our own self-sufficiency is part of the kind of weakness that religion is. 'A third quality is the capacity which children have for open and direct relationships . . .' (p. 94) He believes that this quality of openness lies among the roots of faith. It is to this basic condition of openness that we now turn .

Every man, because he is created by the living God, has at the core of his being the capacity to love, to move outwards towards another, to establish community. He has the gift of divine life already in him. Man,

---

(29) ibid. p. 47

someone said, is the heart of God, because he is the visible expression of God's love. (cf. Ch. 1.1, 1.2)

This is the love that God continues to express every day in the soul of every child – in his experiences, his imaginings, his creations, his wonderings and his responses. And this is so because 'the Word became flesh' – God became a child with all that childhood entails, and he grew painfully into manhood with all the stages peculiar to that state, stages to be reached and transcended only with much suffering. Since Christ entered human history, all that is human has been given its full value; from the tiny baby to the very old, the mystery unfolds itself. (cf. Ch. 1.3)

We have seen just now that in reality the child is already the man in that right from the beginning he is in possession of the value and depth implied in the name of man. As he grows up the child, in his openness, moves towards a deeper realisation of who he is. He is already the unique indivdual with a name of his own. The awareness of this uniqueness is often particularly intense as the child moves towards adulthood. An American youth wrote 'I've put my name up everywhere. There's no place I can go without coming across it. Sometimes on Sundays, I go to the subway station at the corner of 7th Avenue and 86th Street and I stay there all day long just watching my name go by.'[30]

The following passage from *The Child in the Church* sums up much of what we have been saying: 'In the light of the Incarnation, childhood can no longer be regarded as merely a provisional and preparatory episode. The childhood of Jesus does not allow the Church any understanding of childhood that measures the child by what, not yet being adult, he lacks. Jesus was a child. This forbids our beginning exclusively with some definition of what a Christian should be in terms of what a Christian *adult* should be and then planning only *what* must be done to turn the child into the man. Our theology of childhood concentrates on the 'continuous now' of the child's life, just as we emphasize the 'now' of adult life, without neglecting what the child and the adult will some day become. A child at any age may be wholly human and wholly God's. Because Christ was a child, a child can be a Christian.'[31]

Rahner returns to his basic theories on self-transcendence under God's self-communication in the following paragraph. 'Childhood is openness. Human childhood is infinite openness. The mature childhood of the

---

(30)   UNESCO *Courier – Year of the Child Issue* (H.M.S.O.: 1979)
(31)   *The Child in the Church* (op. cit.) art. 38

adult is the attitude in which we bravely and trustfully maintain an infinite openness to all circumstances and despite the experiences of life which seem to invite us to close ourselves. . . . When human childhood finds the courage to be true to its absolute essence, when it realises its own nature as an openness that is unconditional and infinite, then it moves on to a further stage, projects itself by a process of 'transference' to the ultimate consummation of its own nature, to the childhood of man before God. . . .[32]
This notion finds a more personal expression in the following words —'I believe that the child has a wholeness. Looking back, it seems to me that I was whole in the sense that I was not yet disturbed by the sorrows that came later, at school. I was *open*, therefore, to receive. That simple wholeness is something like the wholeness of an animal, but more conscious perhaps. I would compare that simple wholeness with the more complex wholeness that you work towards slowly. I think I am much more whole today at 81 than I was at 40. And perhaps when a new wholeness has been achieved out of the complexities of life, one will be able to see the world invisible again.'[33]

The Eternal Child
'And I know now that youth is a gift of God, and like all His gifts, carries no regret. They alone shall be young, really young, whom He has chosen never to survive their youth. I belong to such a race of men. I used to wonder: what shall I be doing at fifty, at sixty? And of course I couldn't find an answer, I couldn't even make one up. There was no old man in me.[34]
We already mentioned that there is an eternal quality about childhood. We meet and possess our childhood more fully in adulthood, and forever in eternity. '. . . provided we reverently and lovingly preseve this state of our being delivered over to the mystery, life becomes for us a state in which our original childhood is preserved for ever; a state in which we are open to expect the unexpected, to commit ourselves to the incalculable — a state which endows us with the power still to be able to play, to recognise that the powers presiding over existence are greater that our own designs, and to submit to their control as our deepest good.'[35]

---

(32) RAHNER, K. (op. cit.) p. 49
(33) ROBINSON, E. (op. cit) p. 52
(34) BERNANOS, G. *Diary of a Country Priest* (Collins: 1956) p. 347
(35) RAHNER, K. (op. cit.) p. 42

This carrying forward of the child in each of us is essential for the wholeness of the individual man or woman. It must never disappear, for if so, man will have strayed from his beginnings and from his centre; he will risk losing a sense of wonder, of openness and of gift; he will lose sight of his own uniqueness as a child of God. 'Of such is the kingdom of heaven.' (Mt. 19, 14) Christ was aware of the carefree heart of the child who is not conscious of being a receiver yet ever open to receive. The child somehow knows that he has nothing of himself on which to base any claim to gift or favour, yet still believes that love will reach out and enfold him. Perhaps it was this quality of openness in the sinners of his time that drew Jesus to their company. Devoid of pretentiousness, and full of trust, they had ceased to continue the endless quest for self-justification. The lack of the false ambition to be forever in a 'state of grace,' of the drive towards spiritual power and of a self-destructive self-sufficiency was evidence of the eternal childhood still within them. Here lies the freedom and joy of the sons of God. The eternal child at play in the presence of the Spirit teaches the Christian to say '. . . we shall be gay because we shall be openhearted and openhanded, for we shall know, in the depths of our hearts, that what we are and have is not ours but God's, and shall be glad to know it; we shall be gay with all the new-found gaiety of the child re-born within us, the child who has everything to enjoy and love and nothing to lose; we shall be gay because we shall know that we are no longer in the darkness, that spring has replaced the spirit's winter, the 'rains are over and gone', and that if we are faithful, we live, not only now, but for ever and ever, in the Light that is life everlasting.'[36]

5.6 The new Design as a Modern Apologetics

a) Understanding and evaluation on the part of the pupil play a central part in these sketches for a new curriculum. The present plan encourages the pupil to explore and investigate all human experience, especially those we call 'depth-experiences', particularly his own, as a preliminary to his considerations of the concepts, feelings and activities of the Christian religion which are put forward as interpreters of those experiences.

The generally accepted three-fold framework of ideas, feelings and

---

(36) VANN, G. *The Divine Pity* (Collins: 1945) p. 47

actions[37] are identified largely within the three areas of Christian scripture, liturgical celebration, and doctrine. These three areas, among others, are seen as the extension into time of the final revelation that Christ, in himself, constituted, and they purport to illuminate and transform the meaning of human experience for each pupil just as Christ's own humanity revealed the meaning of all humanity.

The truth-claims put forward here follow on the claims made earlier regarding the nature of the Incarnation, (cf. Ch. 1). Just as the incarnation of Jesus Christ is believed to be the revelation of the meaning of the first creation, its 'completion and fulfilment'[38], so Christian revelation today, as partly summed up in the three dimensions (above) should, for the Christian pupil, interpret his life as he grows and suffers and becomes more (or less) human.

b) The Incarnational approach to a new curriculum design holds that the Christian message explains, purifies, intensifies and multiplies the significant experiences of mankind (cf. Ch. 2). These four claims are verified by the understanding, experiencing and evaluating of the transforming influence exerted on human life by the truths, scriptures and sacramental activities of the Christian presence in today's world. Abraham Heschel wrote 'I was born a man and now my task is to become human.'[39] The attraction of Christianity, in apologetical terms, lies in its ability to provide evidence for its role in facilitating and affirming that becoming. Revelation provides a new consciousness for each man as it confirms what his very own nature as a member of the human race strives to tell him, but cannot ever, unaided, completely succeed in spelling out.

He is already in the image of his Maker, born of a mysterious love and a creature of unutterable beauty, who grows into fullness through releasing the creative powers in his fellow man. In brief, the mystery of the Incarnation *explains* human experiences by revealing that in them God is present to human life. Only through his own life-situations can man touch God. The presence of the God-man to life, as caught up and perpetuated into the future, in the total tradition of the Christian church, is presented to the pupil for his free and rational consideration and assessment.

Revelation *purifies* human experience in that it insists on the universal need of redemption. Even the experience of 'the holy' is ambiguous.

---

(37) *A Groundplan for the Study of Religion* (op. cit.) p. 20
(38) *DOCUMENTS OF VATICAN COUNCIL II: Dogmatic Constitution on Divine Revelation* (art. 2)
(39) cf. MORAN, G. *The Present Revelation* (Herder & Herder: 1972) p. 75

The human condition, even in its most pure form, is highly vulnerable. The Christian message enables a man to be analytical and critical of his own deep experiences discerning in them what is for life and what is for death. (The emphasis here should serve to eliminate any strains of pantheism or unacceptable humanism that may be seen as a threat to the uniqueness of Christian revelation.)

Revelation, finally, *intensifies and multiplies* man's life-affirming experiences through contact with the main dimensions (above) of the Christian presence, but chiefly, perhaps, through its understanding of cult, ritual and sacrament. In the liturgy, for instance, the mysterious presence of the call to meaning and freedom within man's daily exist-ence is manifested in full consciousness and celebrated in solemn ritual (cf. Ch. 1.6). What is already at work in the heart of each creature is al-lowed to come forth, is given voice and explicitly consented to, even when he knows that the most radical consent demanded of him, the one disposed over by God and real life, is enacted perhaps mostly outside the cultic celebration (cf. Ch. 4.2). Sacramental celebration is an attuning of the pupil's spirit, an adjusting of the human sensitivity, so that the God who is love can be identified and recognised in his most real presence – that of the community experiences of each man and of the world of men in gen-eral. This presence is grasped and anticipated in cult, ritual and loving community celebration. In all kinds of education 'discovery, like surprise, favours the well-prepared mind.'[40] Hence the claim that revelation intensifies and multiplies the key experiences of mankind. (cf. Fig. 3)

5.7   A Consideration of Objectives

The overall aim in the Incarnational approach to R.E. is, as we have seen, concerned with the initiation of pupils into the worthwhile activity of reflecting in depth on their own and others' experience, and then with encouraging them to understand and evaluate, in freedom, the manner in which the Christian claims that revelation brings significance to these ex-periences works out in practice, developing in them a sense of their own dignity, identity and worth. The suggested sequence of stages in the actual

---

(40)   BURNER. J. *The Act of Discovery* in *Readings in the Psychology of Cognition: eds. Anderson, R. and Ausubel, D.* (Holt, Rinehart & Winston: 1965) p. 607

development of the theme within the new design will generally follow the pattern of the main aims.

1.   This will usually entail the exploration, the investigation and the reflection in depth of some aspect of human experience and the following list of objectives seems appropriate to this stage:-

a) To provide the pupil with an opportunity to i) practise the skill of reflecting on his own experiences at depth; ii) develop insight into himself and his feelings; iii) develop insight into other people and their feelings; iv) develop insight into what constitutes a distinctly human relationship between self and others.[41]

b) To provide the pupil, through a), with the knowledge that his own particular experience is but a part of a more universal phenomenon.

2.   Since revelation in fact only truly happens when human experience is personally perceived in a new light because of it, the objectives in the second movement of the Incarnational approach to curriculum planning would include:

a) an appropriate knowledge of relevant areas of the scriptures and of scripture study with a view to achieving an understanding of how these writings, in testifying for ever to the total humanity of the God who became flesh, testify too to the eternal value of all fleshly experience;

b) an appropriate knowledge and experience of worship and liturgical celebration with a view to achieving a deeper understanding of how the sacraments express, celebrate and intensify the new humantiy of the whole world and thus, of the pupil's new consciousness of the worth and dignity of himself and his experiences;

c) an appropriate knowledge of relevant areas of Christian doctrines with a view to achieving an understanding of how these truths interrelate with and enlighten the previously explored experience; (cf. Fig. 3)

d) a mastery of the skills and techniques required on the part of the pupil to apply these and other elements of revelation to all the experiences of his own and other people's lives both now and in the future.

3.   The authors of this new design are most anxious that the objectives of the evaluation procedure, already mentioned in the general aim of this approach, yet so rarely identifiable in many R.E. programmes, should be given much consideration. The evaluation envisaged here is obviously not an exercise in testing or judging the impact of the curriculum, as a whole, from the outside. This, of course, has its place and will have to be entered

---

(41)   GRIMMITT, M. (op. cit.) p. 57

into, once any pilot schemes are in the schools. What is regarded as important here is the provision of skills for the pupil enabling him to evaluate the
claims of the religion under consideration in terms of the earlier stages of
the curriculum programme with its emphasis on experience and understanding. The pupil is encouraged to ask, and left free to investigate in a
structured fashion, whether or not the Christian claim that revelation
colours and enriches human experience holds true both from the point of
view of community growth in general in the history of Christianity and
of personal relevance in his own situation, e.g., is there evidence that the
Christian revelation fulfills its truth-claims to explain and interpret the
experiences of the faith community and of the individual within this community?; does the understanding, experience (and acceptance) of the
normative areas of revelation within the Christian tradition (mainly, the
doctrines, the scriptures and the celebrations) achieve the communal and
personal fulfilment that is promised?

5.8   The Place of 'Knowledge' in Curriculum Planning

Understandably, much anxiety is expressed about the necessity of 'sheer
knowledge' and factual information in the kind of framework that is here
advocated. Most of the more traditional patterns of R.E., as traced in the catechisms, agreed syllabuses, and in many contemporary outlines for Church
and L.E.A. school programmes, have been centred upon the acquisition of
knowledge. Interest has usually been focussed on the need to 'cover' the
most important areas of 'truths, mysteries and facts,' and on the stages of
the programmes in which each item should be introduced. Perhaps the dis-
tiction between 'knowledge as possession' and 'knowledge as potential' has
not been sufficiently clarified. One can seek knowledge in order 'to have
more' or 'to become more.' As an academic pursuit no one can deny the
importance of acquiring a mastery over all that pertains to detailed information concerning the many-faceted components of any given religion. In
terms of R.E. within the Incarnational approach, however, the selection of
'relevant knowledge' must be guided by the wider considerations of the
pupil's readiness and capacity for 'becoming what he knows.' For that
reason, those who are working on the proposed curriculum-design are prepared to investigate the thinking behind what is known as the 'dialectical
curriculum model' as well as the merits of the more traditional models
already referred to (cf. Ch. 5.3).

The thinking behind the present design recognises that the understanding of a⁺ faith (especially one's own) is impossible without a deep knowledge of relevant information about the dimensions of that faith, but equally recognises that the arbitrary awareness of such facts is, in itself, not sufficient. To have truly educative value for the pupil, for reason and revelation to meet harmoniously in his consciousness, their significance in terms of human experience must be established, understood and evaluated.

Along the lines of Phenix's exposition of the educational value of his 'realms of meaning' (cf. Ch. 3), this design endeavours to integrate knowledge and relevance, information and meaning, in such a way as to enhance the total impact of the experience-based programme on the full personality of the pupil.

> Knowledge and wisdom, far from being one,
> Have oft-times no connexion. Knowledge dwells
> In heads replete with thoughts of other men;
> Wisdom in minds attentive to their own.
> Knowledge a rude unprofitable mass,
> The mere materials with which wisdom builds,
> Till smooth'd and squar'd and fitted to its place,
> Does but encumber whom it seems t'enrich.
> Knowledge is proud that he has learn'd so much;
> Wisdom is humble that he knows no more.[42]

The proposed philosophy of the curriculum for R.E. is intended as a general guide to the fulfillment of human existence through the understanding and evaluation of the Christian religion. Together with Phenix we see it as a contribution to what James Harvey Robinson calls 'the humanising of knowledge'. The encapsulated fruits of professional scholars' study are often beyond the comprehension of the layman, and more so, of the pupil, even though he may be intelligent and enthusiastic. More significantly, this knowledge generally appears to have little pertinence or relevance to the vital concerns of any except those who are professionally commited to it. But there is a great need, Phenix reminds us, for the best insights of civilization (and in the present context, Christian civilization) to be made available to people generally and for its humane significance to

---

(42) COWPER, W. *A Winter Walk at Noon: Bk. VI* in *The Poetical Works of William Cowper* (Oxford Univ. Press: 1934)

to be made clear. 'Popular culture,' he writes, 'need not be mediocre and trivial.'[43] Conversely, if theological and scriptural studies are not communicable or capable of being mediated within the terms of general R.E., then they belong to the realms of esoteric discourse, justifiable indeed as an academic pursuit, but hardly appropriate to the truth-claims already referred to, namely that the Christian religion brings the power of meaning into each young person's life. To paraphrase Phenix a little we may conclude this section by affirming that the present philosophy of the curriculum is dedicated to the proposition that the finest treasures of Christian tradition *can be so mediated* as to become a common inheritance of persons who are seeking to realise their essential humanness (cf. Bruner's reference to the necessity of rewriting and revamping existing subject-matter in Ch. 5.13). What must be avoided here is any suggestion, in the educational process, of opposition between subject-matter and self-realisation. In *The Child & the Curriculum* J. Dewey argues that the child's 'present experience' and the stored experience of the past (knowledge, for instance) each contains the essential elements of the other, they are 'initial and final terms of one reality.' The content of the curriculum should assist in 'freeing the life process for its own most adequate fulfilment. In section eleven of this chapter we briefly touch on the question of the development of doctrine in the effort to clarify the intrinsic relationship between dogma and experience. (For a fuller discussion of these points cf. Ch. 2.2, Ch. 3.3) Dewey sums up a central tenet of the Incarnational approach to a curriculum design when he emphasises 'the need of reinstating into experience the subject matter of the studies, or branches of learning. It must be restored to the experience from which it has been abstracted. It needs to be psychologised; turned over, translated into the immediate and individual experiencing within which it has its origin and significance.'

5.9 The Life Theme in the New Design

The exact nature of the 'life-theme' is by no means clear. The exponents of many recent approaches to R.E. have, at one time or another, claimed it as a suitable medium for the achievement of their objectives. It is our contention too, that the nature and aims of the Incarnational approach are well

---

(43)   GOLDBY, M. et al. (op. cit.) p. 150

served by life-theme teaching. But it seems to us, in the light of the many permutations through which this approach to R.E. teaching has passed in its twenty years of existence, (chiefly because of an understandable non-awareness by curriculum planners of the fact that the life theme, in its purest form, as a method, commits the teacher to a specific theological stance — in the case of Christianity, a precise incarnational interpretation) that each person responsible for R.E. design in any given situation should regard life theme teaching in the light of the theology he holds to be central to the educational requirements of the particular religion under consideration. Otherwise there will be innumerable 'category mistakes' in the sincere 'follow through' of this approach, where themes 'go wild' and 'go to seed' as Hull points out[44], where the position of the sacred vis-a-vis the secular is continually confused.

What ought to be avoided is, on the one hand, a view of the life theme which holds human experiences and contemporary situations to be initial sources of interest for the pupils, whereby religion is linked with life in a well-intentioned yet superficial fashion; on the other hand, a view of the life theme which holds the exploration into human experience to be in itself and without special or normative revelation, an activity which discloses the religious dimension of that same experience.

What is maintained in the Incarnational approach is that the life-theme provides neither a 'pre-evangelising' focus for the subsequent investigation of explicitly religious themes, nor a self-contained locus of 'implicitly' religious values requiring no further explication. Rather, this approach seeks to maintain, within the life theme method, the integrity of the 'sacred' and the 'secular' elements of experience, such that the concrete experiential is adhered to absolutely, without any inauthentic 'leaps' into the abstract, non-experiential. We hold this view because of our contention that the experience explored in the life theme constitutes the basic condition for normative revelation which can be mediated only *in terms* of that experience: that there must be an *instrinsic relation* between the specifically religious dimension and the pupils' life experience. (cf. Ch. 4.2) That is why, in the life theme as we conceive it, the intial exploration into human experience — whether it be vicarious, contrived or personal — is not to be regarded as any kind of preamble to some central religious input, but is, in itself, the necessary locus that is refined and purified, enlightened

---

(44)   HULL, J. *Theology of Themes* (in Scottish Journal of Theology, No. 25: 1975) pp. 20–31

and humanised by the new creation of love as revealed in Christ. (The technical framework in educational terms for this basic conviction was mentioned in Ch. 5.4, 5.6, 5.7)

5.10 A Theology For the Life Theme

The claim that the interpretation, purification and enrichment of the ordinary and intense experiences of each pupil, which may or may not follow on from the examination of, and reflection on, these same experiences in the light of revelation belongs primarily to one particular view of Christian faith — a view which insists that the divine life can be identified at the heart of the becoming and unfolding that goes on in each person and in the world itself (cf. Ch. 1 & 2). Cut off from its life sources, the life theme dies. With no spring to ensure nourishment and growth, it becomes muddy and stagnant. For this reason the definitions and justification for the 'Existential approach' and 'Life-centred R.E.' can never be amputated from their incarnational source. Most schemes, (including many Church-school approaches to R.E.), still have a dualistic structure where the pupils' human experience is considered as a means of clarifying the nature of spiritual or religious life. But the sacred and the secular are no longer 'over-against' each other, as though the divine were a counter-attraction to the human. The strange knowledge that has surfaced into humanity in Christ is that since God has planned, and then assumed, the very stuff of human nature in all its weakness, sinfulness and growing pains as the only and unique expression of his own reality and self-communication, then all aspects of the world and of life contain within them the tangible flesh of the Word of God. If the work of God was to flesh his Word, then the educator in Christianity will endeavour to reveal that Christians are forever engaged in the task of wording the flesh once again.

For many centuries we have been using a kind of language and set of concepts in terms of which the secular means that which is not the holy. The heart of this study contains a plea to shift our images and vocabulary, and interpret the secular (in this case the independent autonomy and total humanness of the pupil) in terms of emergence and identity, and conceive of Christianity as the force and grace which will enable and compel the secular to be itself. By being itself, we now know, it has already, in Christ, become God, because by being itself it is sharing in the only non-symbolic attribute that we can posit of God. The salvation offered by revelation is the protection from all powers that diminish and destroy the truly human and that impose a priori forms (even, and especially, when considered to be religious) that dissolve realities and inhibit growth. The only saving grace that Christianity can bring to religious education is that of identifying the infinite possibility for becoming within the child, and of affirming its presence by providing the spirit-filled, secular milieu for its safe emergence into free and total self-possession. It is central to the thesis at the heart of the Incarnational approach that only a religious spirit, and one in deep contact with modern renewal, can both propose this new project and live successfully through it. There is little indication, as yet, of its whereabouts. This religious spirit 'must surrender many of its ancient images of a mechanical absolute and live much more in the presence of an Absolute who moves things by communicating interiority and wishing to man, who moves man by man's own wishes. We must construct a more complicated dialectic of the human than the romantics were capable of, a dialectic which will know that all inwardness is also a grace and a gift from the outside, from an outside that is neither pusher nor enemy. It is we men who have concocted the idea of the outside as an enemy. As though God could not abide the anthropological.'[45]

The implications of all this for R.E. must not be construed as a premature conversion to current fads or an abandonment of Christian principles in the face of secularist philosophy or pantheistic theology. 'There will, instead, be a realization of what is implied for education by a developed theology of the secular. We have seen that the letting be of being is not so easy as it may sound. On a personal level it means confirming people in their own best possibilities. We know all too well that each of us, to varying degrees, does not wish to become the person he is. We cling to something else. Something finite tends to become divinized; a social fiction is taken seriously; history gets turned into ideology. Christianity, for its part, is to be an idol-smasher that keeps the future open to all the human possibilities; it is to punch holes in the games people play. Twentieth-century movements support the view that the secular world will not remain secular without belief in God. Not any old god will do. It must be the God of the present and the God of the future, the one who meets us in Jesus Christ.'[46]

---

(45)   LYNCH, W. *Towards a Theology of the Secular*: (Theology Digest, Vol. XI., No. 3: 1967) p. 178
(46)   MORAN, G. *Vision and Tactics* (Burns and Oates: 1968) p. 27

5.11 Structure and Sequence in the Life-Theme

These paragraphs suggest some considerations for the development of the structuring and sequencing of a thematic presentation, in terms of the relationship between the exploration of the pupils' experience and its review in the light of revelation. The evaluation by the pupil of the total content and of the truth claims within it, is seen as an integral part of the whole exercise.

1. An *experience* may be either first hand or second hand. It can be selected either by providing an immediate setting through simulation and role-play, by recalling a past experience using pictures and questions, or by suggesting a vicarious experience with reference to stories, films and television programmes.

The experience in question is then enlarged upon by relating it to similar experiences in other people's lives. As well as developing insight and sensitivity, this exercise serves the double function of universalising the experience for the pupil and where necessary, removing the anxiety of the particularity of that experience in his own situation. (cf. Ch. 5.7) Through discussion and creative writing, art, drama, music and role-play, the meaning of the selected experience is explored and examined. The ability to reflect sensitively on human experience can neither be forced nor assumed to be present in pupils at various levels of awareness. 'In some people, a feel for certain qualities of the human condition, such as its transience and mystery, may be arrived at intuitively and exist from an early age. More commonly such insight is the result of later reflection upon experiences such as birth, death, growth, love and friendship. This reflection will be assisted by the acquisition of certain skills which enable the individual to generalise from particular experiences and to handle abstract concepts. Religious education seeks to encourage this reflective activity, to foster the formation of personal convictions and the capacity both to maintain and, where necessary, to modify them in the light of experience.'[47]

2. The experience selected from the child's life is now reviewed in the light of *revelation*. In the perfectly integrated person of Jesus Christ all aspects of the Christian's life are made meaningful by love; they are explained and purified they are intensified and multiplied. With the incarnation, the

---

(47) H.M.INSPECTORATE: *Working Paper on Curriculum 11-16* (D.E.S. Issue, Elizabeth House, 1977)

true signficance of existence entered the world. Sacred Scripture can then be regarded as the original and normative testimony to the meaning of experience. In Liturgy, the true meaning of creation and each one's personal destiny is affirmed and celebrated anew. Doctrines and dogmas represent the efforts of the spirit-community to express the inexpressible and to formulate verbally, for different people in different ages, some of the revealed wisdom of the Spirit concerning the purpose and significance of existence. A brief word now on each of these three dimensions of revelation. (cf. Fig. 3)

a)   'When the Christian in any time or place confesses his faith, his confession turns into a narrative. When the Christian observes Christmas or Easter, in either case it is with reference to a story of things that happened.'[48] The story of Christianity is the history of a people comprising real individuals who live out and struggle with the complexities and richness of humanity. Scripture stresses the active experiences of people and the responses of individuals in community to the person and significance of Christ. Sallie TeSelle observes that Scripture records 'the experience of coming to belief,' the dawning realisation that resurrection is indeed a truth available to all; the gospel expresses the emerging insight that the story of Jesus is *the* paradigm of all human movement.[49]

        Truths which touch man most intensely invariably express themselves in story-form, not necessarily fictional, but certainly in narrative or poetry. Scripture is the story par excellence of Christian faith, and occupies a distinctive position in the development of a life-theme. It should help to move the child towards an integration of his own thought and life. Biographies and autogiographies should always ultimately focus in on one's *own* life. 'Whatever is communicated must come with immediacy, intimacy, intensity and involvement. In other words, in the midst of whatever other questions are raised, one always first and foremost raises the question of oneself.'[50] The stories of Scripture then function as necessary vehicles for the child's self-understanding and the integration of his experiences into the overall pattern of his personality.

b)   In Chapter One we presented a brief outline of the Copernican revolution in our understanding of the liturgy. Instead of an intellectual and spiritual movement from the sacramental event towards its effect in the

(48)   WILDER, A. *Language of Gospel* (Harper & Row: 1964) p. 67
(49)   TESELLE, S. *Speaking in Parables* (S.C.M.: 1975) p. 139
(50)   ibid. p. 146

world, what we now have is a spiritual movement of the world towards the sacrament. Karl Rahner distinguishes between what he calls the 'liturgy of the Son' and the 'liturgy of the world.' 'Throughout the whole length and breadth of the colossal history of birth and death, a history on the one hand full of superficiality, folly, inadequacy and hate – and all these 'crucify' – a history, on the other hand, composed of silent submission, responsibility unto death, mortality and joy, heights and sudden falls; throughout all this there takes place the liturgy of the world. The liturgy of the Son then, (that which we normally call liturgy) is the culmination of that first liturgy, the liturgy of the world.'[51] In R.E., liturgy must not be explained or celebrated in terms of sacred actions that separate pupils from the daily circumstance of life. Since the primary means of grace is always and everywhere human life, Christian liturgy is rather the celebration of the deepest dimension of this human life which is God's self-communication to men. 'The otherness of God is not accessible at the edge of human life at the threshold of another world, but at the very centre of life where men are summoned and graced to create their future.'[52] An R.E. programme which deals with a liturgy that does not open out on all the situations of a pupil's life has seriously misunderstood the basics of liturgical celebration. 'Unless the Christian life in the world is understood to lead organically to liturgical expression, the nature of Christian morality is not grasped either.'[53] Having pointed out that for all men, encounters with their fellow men are the sacrament of their encounter with God, E. Schillebeeckx adds that therefore liturgies are not constructed or manufactured to suit an occasion, 'they develop organically from a renewed spirit.'[54] The final chapter will indicate how central this understanding of liturgy is to experience-based teaching.

c)   Far from being the object of faith, doctrine, like sacred scripture and liturgy, is always a second-order affair. 'A teaching of the Church, even when infallible, is a fragmentary truth which should act as a prod to theologians and faithful alike to begin thinking more deeply on the subject in question. . . . Doctrinal statements are as exposed as scriptural ones to being taken as truths handed down from the heavens without human reception and interpretation. They ought, instead, to be seen as means to prevent

(51)   RAHNER, K. *Secular Life and the Sacraments:* (*11*) (The Tablet, Vol. 225, No. 6823: 1971) p. 266
(52)   BAUM, G. *Man Becoming* (Herder & Herder: 1970) p. 76
(53)   MORAN, G. *God Still Speaks* (Burns & Oates: 1967) p. 106
(54)   SCHILLEBEECKX, E. *Christ the Sacrament* (Sheed & Ward: 1963) p. 262

misunderstandings and as objectifications of what has been assimilated in the Church's experience. Given that context, their inherent limitations will also be apparent.'[55] Doctrine assumes an importance out of all proportion to its true function when it is separated from mystery and the experience of mystery. Understanding is perhaps, one of the most deeply moving experiences of all and what we call 'doctrines' are, to a large extent, the generally agreed, but by no means fixed, formulations of the many grace-filled moments of insight experienced within the community of believers. They become dry and irrelevant 'signs of orthodoxy' only when they no longer enrich the quality of the believer's life. Doctrines can live only when they serve the mystery of the incarnate spirit. Cut off from their life source, doctrines, like plucked flowers, begin to wither. 'What is first needed by teachers and students is the recognition that their own lives are mysterious, enveloped by the presence of a loving God in the transformed world of nature and other people. What must be striven for by various ways, (one of these being the role of doctrine) is to awaken a sense of wonder and sympathy for persons, a readiness to accept freedom and history, and a desire to delve into the inexhaustible richness of the encompassing reality of man's relationship with God in Jesus Christ.'[56]

3.   The *evaluation* envisaged here concerns itself mainly with the community relevance and personal relevance of the Christian revelation. Where community relevance is concerned, the evaluation is based on responsibility and informed judgement regarding the merits of a particular truth claim using, for instance, psychological, sociological, ethical or philosophical criteria. Similarly, these criteria and others may be taken up in terms of critical reflection and analytical evaluation, this time in terms of personal relevance.[57]

.12   An Observation on World Religions

Any discussion of Religious Education today would certainly be incomplete without reference to those faiths other than Christianity which have shaped and inspired mankind. This is a vast area, and must briefly be noted here in terms of the present theological position with regard to the non-Christian

---

(55)   MORAN, G. (op. cit.) p. 119
(56)   ibid. p. 112
(57)   Schools Council, Groundplan, p. 24.

religions, and its basic implications for the Christian R.E. teacher. Fortunately, the time when Christianity *confronted* the great religious traditions in an attitude of suspicion and condemnation has largely past. This has been due to two important factors. In the first place, there has been a good deal of development in ecclesiological thinking (cf. Ch. 1.5). Following Vatican II the Church has grown increasingly to understand itself as a sacramental community functioning in the service of history and the world. *Dialogue* has replaced dogmatics as the key to the Church/world relationship, and the language of triumphalism has given way to phrases such as 'universal brotherhood' and the 'family of mankind'; 'for all peoples comprise a single community, and have a single origin, since God made the whole race of men who dwell over the entire face of the earth.'[58]

Second, and perhaps more importantly, there has emerged a real recognition of the truth and value residing in the faith-systems of other cultures.[59] Christianity can and must learn from the spirituality of Buddhism, stated the Council, 'rejects nothing which is true and holy in these religions.'[60] Moreover, without denying the real differences between the various religions, Christianity must recognise the most significant denominator common to them all, which gives foundation and motivation to the great faiths and ideologies, namely the genuine quest for goodness, truth and beauty which is itself the activity in man of that part of himself which can never be overcome. 'From ancient times down to the present, there has existed among diverse peoples a certain perception of that hidden power which hovers over the course of things and over the events of human life. . . . Religions to be found everywhere strive variously to answer the restless searchings of the human heart.'[61] Very often too, humanism and atheism can provide valuable insights into the full meaning of Incarnation, by their uncompromising assertion of the uniqueness and dignity of man, which prevents the use of traditional religious ideas such as the 'after-life' and so on, as panaceas for blatantly unjust situations.[62]

In recent times the concept of 'anonymous Christianity' has come to the fore, especially in Rahner's thinking. It would be wrong to use this

---

(58) Vatican II, *Declaration on the Relationship of the Church to Non-Christian Religions*, part I; see also, *Pastoral Constitution on the Church in the Modern World*, chs. 2 & 3

(59) cf. Vatican II, Church in the Modern World, part 22

(60) Vatican II, Non-Christian Religions, part 2

(61) Vatican II, Ibid

(62) Cf. Vatican II, Church in the Modern World, parts 19–21

blanket term as an excuse for our own ignorance regarding the rich diversity of other religious traditions and cultures. Neither should the striking similarities between creation myths, salvation histories, ethical systems and anthropologies, lead us to fear an exploration into them. The more open Christianity is in this respect, the more truly incarnational it becomes, for the character of unity-in-diversity must always be the hallmark of created reality in general and of human experience in particular. 'The growth of communication between the various nations and social groups opens more widely to all the treasures of the different cultures. . . . Thus, little by little, a more universal form of human culture is developing: one which will promote and express the unity of the human race to the degree that it preserves the particular features of the different cultures.'[63]

From the point of view of the curriculum the whole situation can be enormously enriching. It is not our purpose here to examine in detail the methodological problems. Nonetheless, without drawing facile conclusions two points can be made. First, it is certainly possible, while avoiding simplistic parallels, to discover in most of the world's religions the fundamental themes of dying and rising, of suffering, of love and compassion, and of life after death, which might legitimately be incorporated into an R.E. curriculum based on the Incarnational approach. Second, the debate concerning the necessary commitment or objectivity of the teacher in handling other religions, must not be restricted to a debate between the required belief or disbelief of the teacher. We are not here concerned with comparing truth claims as such. It should be perfectly possible to maintain a neutrality in relation to overall personal adherence, simultaneous with a total commitment to the *meaning* of another faith for others. This tension is an absolute necessity if it is sincerely acknowledged that all meanings, truths and values in human life, are incarnate and revelatory aspects of the Whole from which they derive and move and have their being.

.13 Research and the R.E. Curriculum

'The first and most obvious problem,' writes Bruner, 'is how to construct curricula that can be taught by ordinary teachers to ordinary pupils and that at the same time reflect clearly the basic underlying principles of various fields of enquiry. The problem is two-fold: first, how to have the basic

---

(63)   Vatican II, Ibid, part 54

subjects re-written and their teaching materials revamped in such a way that the pervading and powerful ideas and attitudes relating to them are given a central role; second, how to match the levels of these materials to the capacities of students of different abilities in school'[64].

Already it can be seen that the tasks awaiting a research team appointed to design a curriculum for R.E. are truly immense. Once agreement is reached on the basis of a curriculum designed for education in general, then the equally demanding enterprise of structuring a parallel curriculum for R.E. must be entered into. This, in turn, will presuppose some general agreement regarding the nature of R.E. in the Local Authority school vis-a-vis the Church school, and then a clarification of the distinction, within the Church school setting, between 'catechesis' (nurture) in its evangelical sense and R.E. as the rational exploration into the meaning of the faith-experience. Moreover, having established this last-mentioned distinction there still remains the problem of isolating the various theological stances within any given belief-system, together with their concomitant means of communication and educational methods. For instance, a theology of Christianity based on a scholastic philosophy and employing extrinsicist categories of thinking will tend to view the R.E. procedure in terms of imparting a body of knowledge, a 'deposit' of faith, where the pupils assimilate the facts and information about the various 'sources' of revelation as the faith is 'handed on'. On the other hand, an 'incarnational' theology which perceives an integral relation between revelation and life experience will view the educational procedure more in terms of process and development in a dialectical curriculum model where the pupil is seen as unique in his personal growth and becoming, and all the factors involved in this process are recognised and acknowledged as intrinsic to his understanding and experience of a personal and dynamic revelation.

The central ideas offered in this book towards a new design for R.E. are but initial attempts to outline a theology and an educational theory of curriculum planning that may begin a serious piece of research into the nature and shape of an R.E. programme in a Christian milieu, for future years.

---

(64)   GOLBY, M. eta al. (op. cit.) p. 477

Chapter Six

Preliminary Notes for a Work Plan: an example

6.1 Introduction

In a follow up to this book we hope to examine in more detail how the central ideas expressed in it could be applied to schemes and projects on the major Christian feasts, sacraments and beliefs. Its basic thrust would be in the direction of enriching the quality of each pupil's life through a revealing of the love and meaning that the Christian perceives at the centre of all creation. But for this to happen, for instance, the courageous grappling with fear, the self-sacrifice that is necessary for love to grow, the sense of responsibility that precedes maturity, each step of the way must be carefully prepared. What we mean is that if plans, schemes and projects in R.E. that purport to touch on and interpret some of the sensitive growth-points of a pupil's life, from a Christian perspective, are to succeed, then the theological, scriptural and liturgical dimensions of, say, the feasts of Christmas, Easter and Pentecost, or the sacraments of Eucharist, Baptism or Penance, cannot be presumed to be understood by the teacher himself or by the pupils but must be carefully studied and reflected upon in a renewed light. As we have seen in Chapters Four and Five, curriculum designs and teaching methods may often have to be reviewed and revised as well.

The suggestions that follow in this chapter arose from a visit with some teacher-training students to Coventry Cathedral. Incomplete as they are, these first reactions of the students and ourselves are offered as an example of how some of the Curriculum Notes in chapter Five can be reflected in a scheme of work at post-primary level. The eclectic nature of the scheme obviously prevents it from being suitable for any one particular year's programme; it is left deliberately wide-ranging to indicate more fully the *kind* of approach that can be adapted and adjusted by the interested teacher to suit his or her own personal requirements.

The following introductory notes to the sample scheme of work offer some very brief comments on the theological, scriptural and liturgical background with which any teacher embarking on such a scheme should be familiar. We have throughout the book stressed the central place of such an awareness (cf. e.g. Ch. 5.7, 5.11) *A Matter of Death and Life* is firmly based on the Easter mystery in its historical and experiential context. To this we now turn.

6.2   A Matter of Death and Life

Background to the Easter Mystery

1) **Theology**   In spite of being of a more limited value commercially, the festival of Easter is properly the high point of the Christian calendar. Neither is it simply a feast of the Cross. It is a mistake to understand Easter as solely to do with the death of Jesus, for it denies the totality of the Paschal Mystery. Our theology of Easter must be life-oriented too, for the reality of Calvary is inseparable from the reality of Resurrection for Christian faith. D.H. Lawrence saw this clearly enough. 'It is the business of the Church to preach Christ born among men which is Christmas, Christ crucified which is Good Friday, and Christ risen which is Easter. And after Easter, till November and All Saints, and till Annunciation, the year belongs to the risen Lord: that is all the full flowering of summer and the autumn of wheat and fruit. All belong to Christ risen. . . The *resurrection is to life*, not to death. Can I not then walk this earth in gladness being risen from sorrow? Is the flesh that was crucified become as poison to the crowds in the street, or is it a spring blossoming out of the earth's humus.'[1]

This essential balance between death and life is founded first of all on the events and experiences of the first Easter, but also on the inescapable character of human experience in general, which Christ's life, death and resurrection illuminates. (cf. Ch. 1.3) Our existence is shot through with the disappointment of failure and the joy of success, the desolation of loneliness and the fulfilment of friendship, the bitterness of rejection and the warmth of acceptance. The cycle of the year itself reflects the seasonal movement of nature through Autumn, Winter, Spring and Summer, with the strange moments of transformation, of birth and death that occur in the plant, insect and animal world. Unless we apprehend Calvary and Resurrection in this universal and experiential sense, we run a dual risk of imprisoning forever in the past the significance of Christ and the actions and events surrounding him; and of projecting true resurrection for ourselves into the promise of a future event. 'To concentrate on a resurrection

---

(1)   Cited by RICHARDS, H.J. *The First Easter: What really happened?* (Collins/Fontana, 1976), pp. 53-54

in the past or on a resurrection in the future will very effectively prevent most from believing in a resurrection here and now. For the eternal life which is promised by the gospel and proclaimed by the church is not a post-mortem life to be lived later on "in eternity". It is life lived in depth at the present moment, so rich with promise that in it eternity has begun.'[2]

2) **Scripture**   The Resurrection of Jesus has always presented many problems for scripture scholars and theologians. One thing is certain — we should not limit the reality of the risen Christ to an over-literal understanding of the Easter narratives, in the same way that we do not bring out the full meaning of Incarnation by taking the Infancy narratives to be complete fact. Understood rightly, the Resurrection of Jesus constituted an eschatological event, speaking to that quality of man which is able to penetrate the empirical, the factual and the demonstrable, and to arrive at a vision of meaning, embracing yet vastly transcending observable reality. The language employed in scripture and in all subsequent theology, provides the Christian community with the necessary analogies for expressing and communicating God's action in Jesus. Linguistic adequacy remains relative to the mystery of revelation because all our words are symbolic and interpretative. (cf. Ch. 3.2) If we try to analyse in straightforward factual terms the appearances of the risen Christ to the apostles, the story of the empty tomb or the Emmaus incident, we sadly diminish the immense, cosmic mystery of Easter. 'The categories of space and time, the categories of ordinary human experience such as 'seeing' and 'speaking' supply us with a language that is only analogous and approximate when we use it to describe the eschatological.'[3]

     By the same token, however, the life and language of men must always be respectively, the only arena and mode of expression for the indissoluble truth of death and vitality which lies at the heart of all love, and of which the ultimate demonstration is to be found in the Christ event. We are not simply specators at the Resurrection; we are called in our personal and social histories to become involved in it, to participate in a present event and to make it our own. 'Every time I know the forgiveness of others, or know that others are forgiven, I know that life has overcome death. Every time I see barriers falling so that the truth can emerge, however

---

(2)   RICHARDS op. cit. p. 65
(3)   BROWN, Raymond *The Virginal Conception and Bodily Ressurrection of Jesus* (Chapman, 1973), p. 125

painfully, I see life victorious over death. Every time I witness prejudice being broken through, or pity aroused, or hope born in a world which seems to offer so little reason to hope, I am witnessing resurrection.'[4] The writers of the New Testament were fully aware of this truth. Matthew 25, John 12: 24, 1 Corinthians 13, Luke 24: 5, all these and many more references testify to the absolute necessity of discovering the reality of Easter in our lived experience of love and service. 'Through Christ and in Christ, the riddles of sorrow and death grow meaningful.'[5]

3) **Liturgy** This truth has been reflected too since earliest times in the Church's liturgical and sacramental life. In particular, the two primary sacraments of Baptism and Eucharist involve the symbolic and sacramental presence of the Passion. (cf. Ch. 1.6, 1.7) The rich symbols of water with its destructive and life-giving powers, and of bread and wine, with their sacrificial and unifying significance, point up the sacramental immediacy of the Easter event. Paul's Letter to the Romans and the Gospel of John contain many important passages in this respect.

4) **Presentation**   An appreciation of the eternal presence of Easter has considerable implications for its presentation in R.E. We have already noted that the seasons, the movement of natural phenomena, such as caterpillars to butterflies, and seed to harvest, provide ideal thematic bases for teaching. Moreover, at secondary level, the combined sacrificial and rejuvenating character of friendship or marriage, and the frequent growth dimension present in many forms of human sorrow and suffering, offer deep and authentic examples of the meaning of Easter in and for everyday existence. The example with which we close this book, develops the destruction — re-creation motif involved in reflecting on the emergence of a new cathedral from the bombed-out ashes of the old. Here are synthesised the various and necessary elements of human living: the bricks and mortar fact of daily toil and achievement, the constant hope in the value of tomorrow, the unquenchable belief in the transformation of the world, the precarious love which persists at the centre of suffering and death, constituting its ultimate triumph over both. W.H. Vanstone relates his experience of having to construct, as pastor, a new church in a district where there has previously been none; from disillusion and a sense almost of triviality, he

---

(4)   RICHARDS op. cit. p. 62
(5)   VATICAN II. *The Church in the Modern World*, part 22

grows to realise the full implications of the project he has undertaken. To quote him at length might provide a particularly powerful entry into the scheme that follows. 'The outcome of so much thought would not be the emergence of some great work of art or the offering of worship of sublime and unearthly beauty: it would be the provision of a fresh coat of paint on the brick wall behind the altar, or of a decent carpet to deaden the sound of feet. While I could believe that God is glorified in some sublime expression of human creativity, I found it less easy to believe that he was glorified in a freshly painted wall. . . . It was hard to take seriously the proposition that the colour one chose to apply to a brick wall was of importance to Him Who is the source and ground of all being, the Eternal, the Almighty, the Unconditional. . . (Nevertheless), there was a continuity between the Church and the world outside the Church: both were made of the same stuff – of things and people and the actions of people; the Church was of a piece with its environment. Whatever else the Church might be, it was certainly part of material reality. . . . Therefore the Church must be at least as important as the things out of which it was made. . . . It was certainly a part of creation.'[6]

Topic: A Matter of Death and Life

General Aims of Scheme: a) To develop a deeper awareness in the pupils of the pattern of the death-to-life movement that lies at the heart of nature and human development in all its aspects.
b) To show how, in the death and resurrection of Jesus Christ, the Christian finds a love and a meaning in this perennial cycle of suffering and joy.
c) To explain how, in liturgy and worship, the believing community celebrates this revelation of love and meaning that is called the Good News for man.

Sequence of Development:
The pattern in all six units has a common movement. Likewise, the activity suggested in each section is aimed at a consecutively deepening understanding of the one truth. *Unit one* centres around the dream of the man who stood amidst the burning debris of Coventry's old cathedral – a dream

---

(6)   VANSTONE, W.H. *Love's Endeavour, Love's Expense* pp. 22, 25–27

that is now incarnated in the new building of great beauty and inspiration. *Unit two* again begins with an aspect of the Coventry theme and then fans out into the search for evidence that material destruction is very often the setting for the emergence of a truly creative spirit of co-operation and love. *Unit three* tries to establish more definitely, that new life in all shapes and forms comes to be only through a process of struggle and suffering. It is not after but *in* the dying that the seeds of new life find nourishment. Forgiveness is the theme of *Unit four*. Returning again to Coventry we begin with the altar constructed in the ruins of the old building, around which a short ceremony of reconciliation is held each Friday. Only forgiveness can heal hatred and anger. Christ is now presented in *Unit five* as the one who has revealed the full meaning of the overcoming of death and sin. This revelation and salvation was accomplished in his own person, his own death and new life — his Passover. The final section, *Unit six*, is an effort to gather the strands of the topics covered in the preceding five units, into the mystery of the Eucharist. The journey from dis-unity to unity, resentment to forgiveness, death to life, has already been successfully travelled by Christ. This is the ever-present victory that is celebrated in the Eucharist.

Unit One: The Cathedral Will Rise Again. . .

Objective: To introduce the story of Coventry Cathedral and to examine in some depth the central questions concerning the relationship between destruction and new creation that it poses.

Pointers towards Personal reflection and Group activity:

1) Begin with slides of the Old Cathedral, before and after destruction. Briefly recount its history. (Slides and information, books, booklets and leaflets mentioned here are all available from Cathedral offices in Coventry.) Enlarge on this extract from the Souvenir Publication *Cathedral Reborn*: 'When the German Air Force left the coast of France on November 14th 1940, the fate of Coventry and its Cathedral was written in the stars; for it was a brilliant night, a bomber's dream. Towards eight o'clock, the first incendiaries struck the cathedral.

"Soon, the whole interior was a seething mass of flames," wrote the Provost R.T. Howard, "and piled-up blazing beams and timbers, interpenetrated and surmounted with dense bronze-coloured smoke. . . . All night long the city burned, and her Cathedral burned with her — emblem of the eternal truth that, when men suffer, God suffers with them. Yet the tower still stood, with its spire soaring to the sky — emblem of God's overruling majesty and love.

"By early morning the destruction was complete. Every roof was gone, and the whole Cathedral lay open to the sky. The matchless pillars, chancel and aisles were lying on the ground in long piles of broken masonry. . . ." It was as if a thousand years of natural decay had come upon the Cathedral in a single night. But, as the morning grew, and a pale sun caressed the ruins, sounds reached it from a stricken city. The sound of crane and hammer and shovel, cleaving new arteries, of voices shepherding evacuees, of the rhythm of workshop and factory. It was the people of Coventry piecing together their shattered home, making a new future, strengthened by the ordeal they had shared with their beloved Cathedral.'

Discuss with the pupils about the beautiful things that men have destroyed. Are they destroyed for ever? Can something positive grow from disaster? Examples of this; (e.g. positive spirit arising from war, tragedy, famine).

2) Now read these words of the Provost (taken from his book, *Ruined and Rebuilt*):

'As I watched the Cathedral burning, it seemed to me as though I were watching the crucifixion of Jesus upon His Cross. After all the Cathedral was not primarily a church belonging to man; it was the Church of Jesus Christ. That such a glorious and beautiful building, which had been the place where Christian people had worshipped God for five hundred years, should now be destroyed in one night by the wickedness of man, was such a monstrous evil that nothing could measure. It was in some way a participation in the infinite sacrifice of the crucifixion of Christ.

'As I went with this thought in my mind into the ruined Cathedral on the morning after the destruction, there flashed into my mind the deep certainty that as the Cathedral had been crucified with Christ, so it would rise again with Him. How or when, we could not tell; nor did it matter. *The Cathedral would rise again.* . . .

'The new Cathedral is now finished; it stands beside the ruins of the old, and both together declare to the world this immortal truth — that in all human experience united with Jesus Christ, painful and sorrowful crucifixion will issue in joyful and glorious resurrection.'

Again show slides, with music and commentary, this time of the new building, emphasising its shape, size and beauty, its colour, symbolism and atmosphere, the glory, hope and love expressed in the stain-glass, the Tapestry, the Unity Chapel. Focus on the linking character of the porch, between old and new, and the immense glass screen of the West Window, with the same function, standing between the ruins and the new Nave.

3) Why do you think the Provost had the following words in his mind on the morning he walked through the smoking ruins of his Cathedral?

> . . .to comfort all those who mourn, and to give them
> for ashes a garland;
> for mourning robe the oil of gladness,
> for despondency, praise.
>
> They will rebuild the ancient ruins,
> they will raise what has long lain waste,
> they will restore the ruined cities,
> all that has lain waste for ages past.   (Is. vv 3 & 4).

4) Discuss the meaning of these passages and their connection:[7]
   a)   "There was life outside the Church. There was much that the Church did not include. He thought of God, and of the whole blue rotunda of the day. That was something great and free. He thought of the ruins of the Grecian worship, and it seemed, a temple was never perfectly a temple, till it was ruined and mixed up with the winds and the sky and the herbs."[8]
   b)   "Then I saw a new heaven and a new earth; for the first heaven and the first earth had passed away, and the sea was no more. And I saw the holy city, the new Jerusalem, coming down out of heaven from God, prepared as a bride adorned for her husband. . . . And I saw no temple in the city, for its temple is the Lord God the Almighty and the Lamb". (Apoc. 21.1–2, 22).

---

(7)   For a commentary on these extracts cf. ERNST, C. *Multiple Echo* (Darton, Longman & Todd: 1979) Ch. 8, section 1.
(8)   LAWRENCE, D.H. *The Rainbow* (Heinemann: 1915) p. 203

Unit Two: Out of the Ashes

Objective: To explore the ways in which spiritual qualities such as courage, hope, reconciliation and love can sometimes grow from negative situations of aggression, hopelessness and pain.

Pointers towards Personal reflection and Group activity:

1) Recap the saga of Coventry Cathedral. Explain the story of, distribute words of and play *A Church is Burning* (Simon and Garfunkel CBS, 62579). Discuss the thoughts behind this record with reference to Coventry Cathedral. What kind of spirit was set free the night the bombs fell? Why can you not burn or kill that kind of spirit? Would that spirit never have been born if no bombs had fallen on the old Cathedral? Or would the beauty and vision captured in the grace of the new building, the Tapestry, the Windows ever have come to be if the Germans had stayed at home that night?

2) Show pictures of burning Protestant and Catholic churches, the result of extremist activity in N. Ireland. Find details of the result of these acts of violence — the coming together in shocked sympathy of Protestants and Catholics to heal these open wounds.

3) Discuss how in the face of threat, danger or disaster feuds are forgotten and barriers are broken down; e.g. in severe flooding, family enmities are set aside in the interests of mutual co-operation; under the threat of invasion a county will unite to survive; more recently, to economise because of fuel shortage, many have formed new friendship through sharing cars; or members of a family by gathering in just one heated room for an evening often restore the family bond.

4) Talk about the manner in which personal tragedy can bring people to their senses, change their way of life, deepen their courage, reveal depths of the spirit up to then unsuspected. Read an extract from the writings of Douglas Bader and talk about his life; tell the story of Francis of Assisi (Link with soundtrack of Bob Dylan from *Brother Sun, Sister Moon*, if possible); discuss Helen Keller and the intensity of desire within her; Christy Brown, armless, now the author of best-sellers; make a list of the world's greatest composers who were either blind or deaf, artists and musicians who were physically handicapped; athletes, with one or more useless limb, yet becoming Olympic champions.

5) Ask if any help in hospitals, old people's homes, cancer wards; ask if any

are friends with severely handicapped people, blind, deaf or spastic; have any been to Lourdes or a similar place? Try to reveal the connection between suffering and spirit; pain doesn't always bring bitterness or unhappiness; the courage and joy of suffering people is a witness to the presence of a whole new world — the world of the spirit. There is more to life than the enjoyment of the priceless gifts of God in nature through the senses and the seasons; there is the land of vision and hope, freedom and wisdom which can usually be entered only through the gates of some kind of destruction.

6) 'An artist, at first only painfully aware of an utter emptiness and impotence, finds his imagination gradually stirred into life and discovers a vision which takes control of him and which he feels not only able but compelled to express. *That is resurrection*.' 'A married couple find their old relationship, once rich and fulfilling, slowly drying up into no more than an external observance — to the point where it seemed impossible that these dry bones should ever live again. Then a new relationship emerges, one that is deeper, more stable, more satisfying than the old one, with a new quality of life which is inexhaustible because it does not depend on the constant recharging of emotional batteries. *That is resurrection*.' 'People, we say, are never the same again after a severe illness or the premature death of someone deeply loved. Sometimes they do shrivel up and atrophy. But appearances here can be deceptive. Under the devastation of their ordeal, which leaves its deep and permanent traces, one can be aware that they are in touch with a new dimension of reality. They have somehow penetrated to the centre of the universe. They are greater people. They are more deeply alive. *That is resurrection*.'[9] Does this sound a little far-fetched? Write an account of an incident or experience in your past life which at first hand seemed to be destructive and tragic, yet on another level brought a deeper and unexpected satisfaction.

Unit Three: Unless the Grain of Wheat . . . .

Objective: To develop insight into the mysterious and inseparable common factors that permeate death and life, with various examples drawn from growth-moments in nature and human development.

---

(9)   WILLIAMS, H.A. *True Ressurection* (Mitchell Beazley: 1972) pp. 10 & 11

Pointers towards Personal reflection and Group activity:

1) Not only are death and life connected, not only must death come before life can follow, but the seeds of new life are contained in, and only in, the dying. It is not like the demolition of the old before the building of the new; it is not as though Winter is the space between the fall of Autumn and the rise of Spring; only *in* the process of suffering and death does the birth of new life, happen. Recall some experiment from science, or begin with a picture that would lead into any of the following topics. Explore the phenomenon of death and new life in everyday examples; focus on the natural cycle of events.

a) Discuss bulbs, fruit, dead leaves, seedlings, etc. (cf. relevant sections in *Alive in Gods World*).[10]

b) Discuss life-cycles; e.g. the tarantula whose egg is fertilised in the decaying body of the mother: the caterpillar enters a cocoon stage, (like death) to achieve its airborne life as a moth or butterfly: tadpoles have to undergo total transformation to become frogs, etc.

c) Discuss other forms of metamorphosis; e.g. fuel into energy into new form of presence in the atmosphere; old cars into scrap into new machinery; useful things, eventually into rubbish then into a new creation like paper, etc. What do pupils think the poet meant when he said 'If we are ever to love a butterfly we must care for a few caterpillars'. Plan a project showing the decaying process in all living things, and the part it plays in the wider, ever-present thrust of life; gather evidence for this from other subjects (science, botany, physics), from the laboratory experiment, from observation and from experience.

2) Move to a deeper level of consciousness and experience, yet within the students' capacity. Discuss the miracle of a baby beginning to walk, denying the security of staying forever within his mother's arms; of his climbing the stairs for the first time: there is a kind of dying in the first day of school, the first day in the secondary school, the first holiday away from home, or the setting up of a new home in a flat or institution. Talk about the pain and understanding that are part of growing up; the pain of childbirth in the very beginning, leading to life, and the agony of death at the other end, leading to a very new and special kind of life; talk about the denial of selfishness when you enter into a friendship or when you fall in love.

3) 'Margaret O'Neill, a Corkwoman, came to live in packaged, self-contained, cellophane, Loyola St. where people barely said "Good Morning" to each

---

(10)   WADDERTON Group *Alive in God's World* (Church Information Office: 1969)

other. She began to wave at cars. Soon she wasn't saying "Good Morning" but "how are you at all?" Her children started to invite in other children to their house, and after a bit Margaret had set up a relay school service. One evening she passed and Paddy Kelly, who was cutting his grass in front of his house thought to himself, "She changed this street." It can never be the same again. From *Old* street it became *New* St. It was a Passover. From something dull, dead, cold, to something warmer and more human.'

'Or my cousin Agnes, 31, married to Edward — a year older. No financial worries, but not getting on well. Last Saturday week there was a terrible row, and at last they really had it out. Frank, truthful. The session lasted most of the night, but they got on well for a fortnight after it. It was a painful passover experience — this breaking through into a new state of a more truthful relationship. It cost something, as Joe, my next example knows.'

'Joe stuck it out as a bachelor until he was thirty-six. Mrs. O'Brien, his landlady, was so fond of him! "A grand solid boy." She used to have a glass of milk and a chocolate biscuit for him every night, and never once forgot to put a hot water bottle in his bed after the 1st of September. Joe had a good job, his own car, drank a fair bit, and had a gay time. But . . . whatever happened; nobody really knows; Joe sort of fell for Rose. It was an instant marriage and Joe's entire comfortable bachelor kingdom fell in one explosion. It was difficult at first to give up the consolations of bachelor life — the beer and the biscuit. But after marriage he had a new shared and more generous life — if not Rose centred at least Rose tinted. Another passing from death to life through love.'[11]

a)   Compile as complete a list as possible of glimpses of resurrection; i) in everyday life, ii) in poetry and literature, iii) in music and art, iv) in nature. This assignment could be undertaken in groups according to personal interest in the various areas.

b)   In groups, compose a reflection in which one of the following experiences is brought to life: i) night-day, ii) childhood-adolescence, iii) sickness–health, iv) anger–peace. Each group should tape its reflection and present it to the class accompanied by a mime or visual imagery.[12]

4) Read and comment on *Death of a Gardener* by Phoebe Hesketh: or

---

(11)   CROSBY, E. *The Meaning of the Redemption* essay in *Jesus Christ Our Lord* S. Freyne (ed.) pp. 78–9 quoted in *Jesus of Nazareth* (Veritas Publication 1978), *Irish Catechetical Commission* p. 28
(12)   *Irish Catechetical Commission* (op. cit.) p. 29

distribute the words of the following poem and ask if they agree or not: [13]

> I am tired of white beauty;
> daffodils in spring
> sunset on a hill
> a young deer leaping over snow
> blue winds across a blue sea
> crystal as naked as the spirit.
>
> Give me dark beauty;
> a flower half dead
> a grey sky
> a dog that limps
> broken glass and a cut finger
> a swamp where a tree looks
> like an amputee.
>
> Darkness is a special kind
> of light,
> Pain is ebony shining
> like a new sun. *A Special Kind of Light*

Which is the more difficult to bear, having a tooth out or getting out of a friendship? watching a doctor taking out your stitches or watching a falling Autumn leaf at the end of a special summer? the death of your friend or the death of his friendship?

Think of a time in your life when you passed from sorrow and disappointment to joy and trust. Describe (unemotionally) how you felt at the change.

5) What is this author endeavouring to express:

'The sun sets only to rise again, nature dies in the autumn only to revive in the spring, hatred sometimes leads to reconciliation, love grows through conflict that is resolved; animals and plants die, but their substance is absorbed by other living creatures. Good survives by turning the apparent victory of evil into a victory of its own.' 'Birth and Death (are) inseparable

---

(13)   HESKETH, P. *Death of a Gardener* in *Seven Themes in Modern Verse* (Harrap: 1968) p. 65

on earth; /For they are twain yet one and Death is Birth', says Francis Thompson.

'We experience death and rebirth often in our own lives. We pass the test, we overcome the fear, we break through the barriers of shame and timidity, we make progress against our inflexibility and defensiveness, we learn from our mistakes. In fact, we discover with time and experience that progress and growth in the human condition — whether it be personal or social — is always accomplished through a series of deaths and rebirths. In the psychotherapeutic experience in particular, we learn that we can only rise to the new man — the more free, more open, more confident, more authentic self — by dying to the old man, that narrow, anxious, fearful, defense-ridden self. We become more human and society becomes more human and society becomes more just only through death and resurrection.'[14]

Unit Four: To Forgive is to Die a Little

Objective: Through a consideration of the story that surrounds the Altar of Forgiveness in Coventry and its effects around the world, to deepen the pupils' understanding of the demanding and challenging reality of forgiveness.

Pointers towards Personal reflection and Group activity:

1) On the surface, brotherhood and forgiveness look easy. We smile and say we're sorry. we grin and apologise, but forgiveness has little to do with this. Only the great can really forgive because in forgiveness is the demand to accept the ugliness in the other who is trying to destroy us. Sometimes it is only forgiveness that can heal anger and hatred in another. We don't try this too often because forgiving is a kind of dying. But the art of loving is the art of endless forgiveness. Show a large picture or slide of the altar that is built on the site of the old Cathedral in Coventry. It is an altar of forgiveness with the words 'Father, forgive' etched into the wall close-by. On it are two crosses, one of wood the other of nails, both fashioned from material salvaged from the burnt-out ruins. Around this altar, at 12.00 every Friday a ceremony of reconciliation is held when the city once again remembers its promise to go on forgiving. (Play *Father*

---

(14)   GREELEY, A. *The Great Mysteries* (Gill and Macmillan: 1977) p. 43

Forgive Them — Ralph McTell, *My Side of Your Window*: TRA 209). Discuss the difficult challenge that true forgiveness presents.

2) Copies of the following stories could be run off and distributed to the pupils. It might be useful to tape-record the passages and play them to the class while they read them, as they listen.

'In 1941 my mother took me back to Moscow. There I saw our enemy for the first time. Nearly 20,000 German prisoners were to be marched in a single column through the streets of Moscow. The pavement swarmed with onlookers, cordoned off by police and soldiers. The crowd were mostly women. Everyone of them must have had a father or a husband, a brother or a son killed by the Germans. They gazed with hatred in the direction from which the column was to appear. At last we saw it. The women clenched their fists. The soldiers and the police had their work cut out to hold them back. All at once something happened to them. They saw German soldiers, thin, unshaven, wearing dirty bloodstained bandages, hobbling on crutches or leaning on the shoulders of their comrades. They walked with their heads down. The street became dead silent — the only sound was the shuffling of boots and the thumping of crutches. Then suddenly I saw an elderly woman in broken-down boots push herself forward and touch a police-man's shoulder saying, "Let me through.' There must have been something about her that made him step aside. She went up to the column, took from inside her coat something wrapped in a coloured handkerchief and unfolded it. It was a crust of black, hard bread. She pushed it awkwardly into the pocket of a soldier, so exhausted that he was tottering on his feet. And now suddenly from every side, women were running towards the soldiers, pushing into their hands, bread, cigarettes, whatever they had. The soldiers were no longer enemies. They were people.'[15]

'As I recall, it was Erich Maria Remarque (author of All Quiet on the Western Front) who once told the following story: During the confusion of an infantry attack a soldier plunges into an out-of-the-way shell hole. There he finds a wounded enemy — either French or English. The sight of the man with his fatal wound moves him so, that he gives him a swallow from his canteen. Through this bit of human kindness a certain brotherly bond immediately springs up between them. The bond becomes deeper as they try to chat a bit. The dying man obviously wants to tell about his wife and children on whom he dwells with his last thoughts. He points to his shirt pocket. Understanding this gesture correctly, the German soldier

---

(15)   YEVTUSHENKO *A Precocious Autobiography* (Dutton: 1972) p. 101

extracts a wallet from it and then takes out a few family pictures. The gaze of the wounded man wanders over them with sadness and infinite love. The German soldier is deeply touched at that; minutes ago he would have stabbed the enemy with his bayonet; minutes ago all of his battle instincts were unleashed, as was natural in an attack. And now one of the enemy lies before him — and is no longer an enemy. No longer is he the Frenchman or the Englishman, he is simply a man, a father and a husband, one who loves and is loved, one who defended his home and who now must bid farewell to everything he holds dear. All at once the German soldier is confronted by that other man in a completely different way. It suddenly becomes clear to him that the friend/foe relationship is by no means the only one, but that behind it, or above it, there is an immediacy to the other person — who lives, as I do, in a house amid loved ones, and who, as I do, has his joys and cares.'[16]

What happened in that shell hole? Did the German soldier suddenly remind himself of his duty to love his fellowman, fight back the ferocity of his battle instinct, and force himself to a gesture of human kindness? No, something quite different occurred. Instead of his having to struggle to change his own feelings, the *other* person was changed for him, and for that reason — and that reason only — *then* changed his own way of reacting. For that reason only, could he love the other person.

Questions such as the following might be asked:-
In our town or city today, what groups of people should begin to seek the forgiveness of others?

The National Organisation for Victims and Offenders (NOVO) is anxious that wherever possible prisoners should meet and be forgiven by those they have offended. Describe how you would feel when confronted by the man who had blinded or crippled you, or severely wounded your friend, or robbed your parents of all they had saved.

3) Antoine St. Exupery was lost for many days when his plane crashed in the desert. This is how he describes his feelings when he was rescued by some Arabs, 'You (Bedouin of Libya) are Humanity, and your face comes into my mind simply as man incarnate. You, our beloved fellow man, did not know who we might be, and yet you recognised us without fail. All my friends and all my enemies marched towards me in your person. It did not

---

(16)   THIELICKE, H. *Facing Life's Questions* (Collins: 1979) pp. 47 & 48

seem to me that you were rescuing me; rather did it seem that you were forgiving me. And I felt I had no enemy left in all the world.'[17]

Is this kind of experience unusual? Could one call it religious? Read and discuss the profound reflections on sin and forgiveness in the encounter between Raskolnikov and Sonia in Dostoyevsky's *Crime and Punishment*.[18]

Unit Five: Destroy This Temple . . . .

Objective: To explain how, for the Christian, the life, death and resurrection of Jesus Christ shed a unique light on the necessary place of forgiveness and reconciliation in individual and community growth.

Pointers towards Personal reflection and Group activity:
1) Christ's passage through death to his Risen Life with the Father is the supreme instance of a leaving behind and going-out to attain a new life of total self-givingness, the life of God. Christ unites men with himself and brings them into the current of his going to the Father, through death to the life of the Spirit. The Christian's life is to be a continual process of denial to self-centredness in order to live more fully Christ's life of love and forgiveness.

Distribute the words of and play, Sydney Carter's Song *Lord of the Dance*. Name some of the people who could have written these words? What famous men have been ridiculed while alive, sometimes killed, and yet their spirit remains alive, the inspiration of many? These men faced death to bring hope and freedom to others — men like Schweitzer, the Kennedys, Luther King, Gandhi. P. Pearse, a poet and patriot, described his ultimate decision in this way:

> I turned my back on the dream I had shaped
> And to this road before me my face I turned.
> I set my face to the road before me,
> To the work that I see, to the death I shall meet.

---

(17)   de SAINT-EXUPERY *Wind, Sand & Stars* (Penguin: 1939) p. 141
(18)   DOSTOYEVSKY, F. *Crime and Punishment* (Penguin: 1951) pp. 330–346

2) Jesus had to set his face towards the tragedy ahead, also, and he put it like this 'The Son of Man will be delivered into the hands of men; they will put him to death; and three days after he has been put to death he will rise again.' (Mk.9, 31). Shocked and unable to understand, his Apostles tried to stop him. But he had his work to do. He would see it through, even if it meant dying. He had given himself to people and to his Father at every moment of his life. He had died many little deaths all his life, as he denied himself to be obedient to the needs of others and the will of his Father. Now he would give his very life.

For his friends this was a tragedy. They had pinned their hopes on him, left their jobs for him, expected wonders from him. But their dreams were shattered, their hopes crushed. He was killed as a criminal on a shameful cross. They were dispirited, disillusioned and despairing. Until they began to understand. They began to see a pattern in his life. They remembered remarks he had made, such as 'Destroy this Temple and in three days I shall rebuild it' or '. . .they will mock him and scourge him and spit at him and kill him; and after three days he will rise again.' (Mk.10, 34). This was the coming of the Spirit; now they could recognise Jesus, his new way of life, the mystery of his death, the meaning of resurrection. 'Their eyes were opened', 'they recognised him', 'their hearts burned', and they spread the news that 'God raised this man Jesus to life, and all of us are witnesses to that. He has made this Jesus whom you crucified both Lord and Christ' (Acts 2, 32–36).

The community of his followers realised that the risen Christ was now with them all the time. Death had produced a new kind of presence in their love for one another, in their mutual forgiveness. Jesus was really risen, transformed in death and present with them and living in them, the inspiration of their lives. As Christ has been raised from the dead, so, too, are all men who 'belong to him'. The sacraments of the Church are the celebration of the good news that Jesus is amongst us, that death is swallowed up in victory (I Cor. 15, 55), that death is not the end but the beginning of the rich, more abundant life promised by the Saviour. The Christian believes that this risen life is his and that the Spirit of Love is living now in the centre of his live. What are the difficulties in this kind of explanation?

3) Do you think that Christians sometimes are over-concerned with sadness and suffering, mortification and dying, forgetting that their faith is really an Easter faith, full of joy and victory and new life? How would you describe your faith?

4) Dramatize a scene or present a mime or dance to suggest the rejoicing of

the Apostles when the news of Christ's resurrection began to dawn on them. It could be a deep quiet portrayal of the Emmaus incident or a care-free celebration of victory to the *Alleluia chorus* from Handel's *Messiah*.

5) What is the Prophet referring to in these lines?

'Only when you drink from the river of silence shall you indeed sing.
And when you have reached the mountain-top, then you shall begin
to climb
And when the earth shall claim your limbs, then shall you truly dance.
For what is it to die but to stand naked in the wind and to melt into the sun,
And what is it to cease breathing but to free the breath from
its restless tides, that it may rise and expand and seek God
unencumbered?[19]

6) What are the implications of the following passage for each Christian's life:
'The best hint of an explanation of the mystery of good and evil to be found in the cross and resurrection of Jesus is that through suffering he came alive. The cross not only preceded the resurrection, in some deep way which we cannot fully understand but which seems to resonate well with our own experiences, it caused the resurrection. By dying with such courage and faith, Jesus, through the help of the heavenly Father, won resurrection. Life not only triumphs over death but somehow flows out of it. Death is not merely a prelude to life in the new man but also a cause; this is a commonplace of psychological growth inside or outside the thera-peutic process. We can only rise if we are willing to go through death, not just as antecedent in time but also as it is precisely the liberation from fear of death that causes resurrection.'[20]

Unit Six: As One Bread That is Broken

Objective: To promote some insight into the manner in which Christians see the Eucharist as a celebration of the continuing presence in the world of an abiding Spirit of love and meaning making true humanity and com-munity always possible.

---

(19)   GIBRAN, K. *The Prophet* (Heinemann: 1926) p. 94
(20)   GREELEY, A. (op. cit.) p. 48

Pointers towards Personal reflection and Group activity:

1) To understand the Christian community and the Eucharist as a sign and cause of it, one must do so in terms of the more readily knowable and experienced communities of family, friends, neighbourhood, and so on. A sense of belonging to, and participation in, a community is necessary to understand what 'union with' means in relation to the Eucharist.

Explore relationships in family life, school life, community life, football teams, societies, pop groups, etc.

Discuss the demands of being a member of a group, of the way one learns to love — the understanding and acceptance, openness and strength, the bearing with weakness, awkwardness, trial and error. Learning to love is learning to be trusting and daring, a facing of reality, a responsible service to others. What kind of spirit must exist within a group if it is to survive?

Describe, in writing, the qualities of the people you would gather to form a group intent on an arduous and prolonged task. Mention the attitude you consider to be the most destructive of community life. Mount a montage of pictures and newspaper cuttings highlighting the successful moments of relationships within a group.

2) In a sermon on the Eucharist, Pope Paul VI said, ". . .(The Eucharist) canonises the perfecting process of mankind that tends towards unification, and simultaneously completes it, preserving for society. . . the spirituality of the individual as well as that of the collective unity. . ." Discuss how Jesus had formed true and really human relationships with his friends before he celebrated the Last Supper with them. Reconsider the list of characteristics of genuine friendship and sharing in community — living and see whether the Eucharistic gathering possesses the same attitudes.

3) Discuss a picture or poster of people celebrating. What are they celebrating? Why? Write a list of these reasons — friendship, growth, thankfulness, beginnings, endings, hope, victory, reconciliation, unity. . . . How many of these reasons are in the Christian Eucharistic celebration? What exactly is the good news that is celebrated? List of ways in which people normally celebrate — singing, eating, drinking, greeting, dressing-up, well-wishing. . . How many of these are discernible in the Eucharistic gathering?
Trace the refrain of forgiveness and peace in the words and gestures of the Eucharistic Liturgy.

8) Find and reflect on the references to unity in Our Lord's discourse at the Last Supper. (esp. John: Chapter 17) Search through the common Eucharistic Prayers for mention of unity, one body, community, members of one head, etc. List the signs and symbols of unity in the whole

Eucharistic action — in one building, around one table, partaking in one meal, one loaf from many grains, one cup of wine from many grapes, one belief in the one Christ into whose Body, Christians believe, all men are being formed.

9) At this point a final evaluation exercise is desirable (as suggested in Ch. 5,11) to determine, to some extent, the pupils' appraisal of the truth claims explored in a scheme such as this, regarding the relevance of Christianity to life.

10) The students responsible for much of this scheme produced a popular 15 min. slide/tape essay that gathered up the key points of the general aims. A similar creative project might well be undertaken by senior pupils at little expense and with much satisfaction.